COPING BETTER ...
Anytime,
Anywhere

COPING BETTER ...
Anytime, Anywhere

THE HANDBOOK OF RATIONAL SELF-COUNSELING

Maxie C. Maultsby, Jr., M.D.

Illustrated by Kathryn L. Burns

Prentice Hall Press • *New York*

Published by Prentice Hall Press
A Division of Simon & Schuster, Inc.
Gulf + Western Building
One Gulf + Western Plaza
New York, NY 10023

PRENTICE HALL PRESS is a trademark of Simon & Schuster, Inc.

Library of Congress Cataloging-in-Publication Data
Maultsby, Maxie C.
    Coping better—anytime, anywhere.

    Includes index.
    1. Rational-emotive psychotherapy. 2. Self-
actualization (Psychology) I. Title.
RC489.R3M382 1987   616.89'14   86-91441
ISBN 0-13-404435-5

Designed by Irving Perkins Associates

Manufactured in the United States of America

10 9 8 7 6 5 4 3 2

DEDICATION

For two important reasons I dedicate this book to Dr. Albert Ellis, who is generally recognized as the father of cognitive-behavior psychotherapy.

First, Dr. Ellis is my highly esteemed mentor and long-time good friend. I cannot thank him enough for personally training me in his world-famous technique of psychotherapy: Rational Emotive Therapy—RET. My training with Dr. Ellis and the exposure he gave me to other pioneers in the cognitive-behavioral field formed the professional foundation upon which I developed the technique of Rational Behavior Therapy (RBT) and the emotional self-help concepts and techniques described in this book.

Second, in the best tradition of the forever helpful mentor, Dr. Ellis interrupted his awesome schedule to give the prepublication manuscript of this book his critical professional analysis.

Last, I also dedicate this book to the many people who allowed me to help them learn to cope better with anybody or anything at anytime. I sincerely believe that you will quickly become one of them.

ACKNOWLEDGMENTS

Many thanks go to Sylvia Wrobel for her helpful contributions to this book and to Kathryn L. Burns for her excellent illustrations. I also want to acknowledge Elizabeth and the Reverend Joseph Stemley of Baltimore, Maryland, for their excellent, helpful comments and proofreading of this manuscript.

Special thanks go to Eleanor Royalty for her commitment to this work, to Julie Logan for her editorial comments, and to Pat Garr for retyping the many drafts of this book so cheerfully.

Very special thanks go to Walter Gaffield. He is absolutely the best copy-editor I have ever had the good fortune to have mark up my manuscripts.

CONTENTS

INTRODUCTION

Congratulations! Reading this book as suggested can be the best thing you ever do for yourself.

Every year, at least one emotional self-help book is on the best-seller list. And if you are like most self-help book readers, you have already read one. It probably prescribed good advice that had helped many people. But did it tell you exactly what was the *best* advice for you in your unique life situation? The answer probably is no; and that's where this self-help book *is* different.

This book was especially designed to be your personal handbook for coping better with absolutely *anything* at anytime in your unique life situations. But like all handbooks, this one only *informs* you. It does not *carry* you. Carrying you to natural happiness and better coping skills is *your* task. Only you can do it. But it's much easier to do than you might think. Just read and follow the clear-cut directions this complete self-help handbook gives you.

You will quickly learn how to cope better with romantic disappointments, job loss, missed "golden" opportunities, actual rejections, fear of rejections, and all of your other self-defeating emotions. You name it; this book will show you how to cope better with it. All you need to do is act logically on these five facts of life:

1. To achieve permanent personal happiness, you must invest a little time and daily effort. So be patient with yourself. The only thing people usually get instantly, the very first time they try, is trouble.

2. You can not learn anything instantly. But if you read this book as suggested, you instantly will start learning to cope better with anything in your life.

3. You will learn fastest and best from this book if you keep an open mind, even about the ideas that "feel wrong" when you first read them. This book always gives you good supporting evidence for its ideas. The chapters follow a logical sequence—each one prepares you for the next. So, to get the best results, be persistent, and look carefully at all the facts and examples.

4. Here's an easy way to ensure that you remember the helpful ideas you learn. Do frequent minireviews. Minireviews are frequent glances at the table of contents of the sections you have already read.

The section content pages were specially written to give you these two benefits: (a) a quick overview of what you are going to learn and (b) a strong reinforcement of your memory for what you have already learned. So do a minireview every time you pick up the book. Those quick reviews will give you the closest thing to 100 percent recall that you can get.

5. Good intentions alone *never* accomplish anything worthwhile. What you actually do is the only important thing. Success at a worthwhile task is like baking a chocolate cake. It doesn't matter at all how much you might want the cake and how hard you might try to bake it; if you forget the chocolate, you will *not* bake a chocolate cake.

The same cause-effect law applies to learning how to cope better with your life. If you omit something, then you cannot get the best results. So do *not* skip anything, not even a word.

SECTION I

Instant Self-Analysis

CHAPTER 1: The Many Good Things about this Book—This chapter will show you how to get the most help from this book in the shortest time possible.

CHAPTER 2: Your Instantly Helpful Self-Analysis—Here you will learn how to give yourself an instantly helpful self-analysis for unnoticed personal factors that keep even the sanest and most intelligent people from coping better with themselves or anything else.

CHAPTER 3: Instant Stress Reduction—This chapter will give you a fast, safe, and reliable stress-reducing maneuver.

CHAPTER 1

The Many Good Things about this Book

Instantly Helpful Insights

Avoid the common mistake of reading a self-help book the way you read a novel—that is, from front to back as fast as possible. That's the best way to read novels because the purpose of novels is to entertain you. The faster you read them, the greater your entertainment per unit of time and personal effort. But this book is not a novel.

This book is the illustrated handbook of instantly helpful self-analysis and behavioral prescriptions for coping better with absolutely anything at anytime. Instead of entertaining you, it shows you the healthiest way to change and direct your life. But this also is enjoyable reading. The main goal, though, is for you to learn how to cope better with yourself and absolutely anything else. That's why, among other good things, this chapter describes the best way to read this book.

Special Vocabulary for Chapter 1

Rational. Any thought, emotional feeling, or physical action that has three or more of these characteristics: (1) is based on obvious fact; (2) best helps people protect their lives and health; (3) best helps people achieve their short- and long-term goals; (4) best helps people avoid their most dreaded conflicts with other people;

(5) best helps people feel the emotions they want to feel without alcohol or other drugs.

Self-Counseling.   Thinking ideas and then reacting to them with the most logical emotional and physical responses.

Thinking.   Mentally processing an idea, then mentally processing other ideas about the first idea to decide if that first idea deserves to be acted upon emotionally and/or physically.

Important Questions Answered in Chapter 1

1. It is safe to let untrained, emotionally upset people counsel themselves?
2. What is Rational Self-Counseling?
3. How can you know for sure if your self-counseling really is rational?
4. What's the best way to make irrational self-counseling rational?
5. What are the especially helpful features of this book?
6. What is the best way to read this book?

THE FIRST GOAL OF THIS BOOK

The first goal is to help you quickly learn how to do Rational-Self-Counseling (RSC). Why? Because RSC is the fastest, safest, and most reliable method of emotional self-help.

A COMMON QUESTION

Is it safe to let untrained, emotionally distressed people counsel themselves? Yes, of course, it's safe; but even if it weren't, emotionally distressed people would counsel themselves anyway. They have to; they have no choice about it. Self-counseling is the *only* means of self-control for everybody. That becomes obvious, once you understand what self-counseling is.

Self-counseling is Thinking ideas and then Reacting to them with the most logical, emotional, and/or physical responses. Thus, self-counseling is the basis for both healthy *and* unhealthy self-control.

It doesn't matter where you get your ideas. You can get them from mental health professionals, parents, churches, newspapers, radio, television, this book, or wherever. But before any idea can influence your emotional feelings or physical actions, you have to *think* it, *believe* it, and then *react* to it in logical, emotional, and/or physical ways.

But thinking, believing, and reacting logically to an idea instantly makes that idea *your* idea. So, as long as you are awake and alert, you will have to counsel yourself. Your only choice will be how you do it.

If you are like most people, you use both healthy and unhealthy ideas in your self-counseling. But if you want to, you can learn how to counsel yourself using more healthy ideas and almost no unhealthy ones.

How can people quickly separate their healthy ideas from their unhealthy ones? *Easily,* if they remember and act on the following three facts: (1) healthy ideas are Rational ideas; (2) unhealthy ideas are irrational ideas; (3) answering the Five Rational Questions for Rational Self-Counseling is the *best* way to see if ideas are rational and therefore healthy.

The Five Rational Questions for Rational Self-Counseling

1. Is my thought based on obvious fact?
2. Will acting on my thought best help me protect my life and health?*
3. Will acting on my thought best help me achieve my short- and long-term goals?
4. Will acting on my thought best help me avoid my most dreaded conflicts with other people?
5. Does my thought best help me feel the emotions I want to feel without alcohol or other drugs?

For a thought to be rational for you, it must deserve at least three honest *Yes* answers from you for those questions. Otherwise, the

---

*The words *me* and *my* refer here to the person doing the rational check of his or her thoughts.

thought will not be rational for you. To cope better, you must immediately replace all such thoughts with rational ones, i.e., ones that do deserve three or more honest *Yes* answers from you to the Five Rational Questions.

Special Helpful Features of this Book

This book follows the three golden rules for rapidly effective teaching. First, it tells you what it's going to teach you. Second, it teaches you. Third, it gets you to rediscover what it has taught you.

So, expect to see *Instantly* useful ideas more than once. And remember, the only thing people usually learn perfectly with just one chance is how to get into trouble. Everything worthwhile requires at least a little repeated mental exposure and practice.

Each chapter begins with helpful insights, followed by a special vocabulary, where it's needed. Most of the words, however, will be common everyday words. You probably know them well already; but their most popular meanings are often so irrationally subjective that they trigger unhealthy reactions. To ensure that your self-counseling is always Rational, use only the objective meanings of words given in the special vocabularies.

In the first part of each chapter you will find important questions that the chapter answers. These questions will increase your concentration and your short- and long-term memory for the many instantly helpful facts. You will also find brief reviews of those instantly helpful facts, plus occasional mnemonic illustrations. The illustrations will also increase your insight, concentration, and long-term memory.

At the end of appropriate chapters you will find memory-aid questions. These questions do not test you; instead, they strongly reinforce your memory for the helpful ideas you will have just learned. So expect the answers to these questions to be easy and obvious; but answer them thoughtfully and thereby increase your instant recall for how to cope better with everything. If you miss more than two of any chapter's memory-aid questions, immediately reread the chapter; then answer all of the questions again.

The Best Way to Read this Book

Starting with Chapter 3, make the remainder of this first reading a fast skim-through. On this skim-through, read only the instantly helpful insight pages at the beginning of each chapter, the special vocabularies, and the lists of important questions that each chapter answers; ignore the memory-aid questions at the end of each chapter.

Actively read the important questions that each chapter answers. By this I mean, have a little mental talk with yourself about each question. For example, one of the important questions answered in Chapter 2 is: "How are YUPI (Your Unhappiness Potential Inventory) items like pollutants in the air we breathe?" People who actively read that question think things like: "How about that? I wonder what he means?"

After little self-talks like that, reading the chapters will make the answers to the questions almost jump off the pages into your permanent memory.

Stop your skim-through at the cover page for Section V. Then schedule at least twenty minutes (but no more than an hour) for your daily self-help reading. It's best to read at the same time every day, or as near to it as possible. Think of these times as your scheduled appointments with the most reliable and effective counselor you can have—yourself. Then be as diligent and prompt in keeping your self-counseling appointments as you would be in keeping appointments with a paid professional. The best and most rapid results come *only* if you give yourself at least that much courtesy and respect.

Once you choose your daily reading time, start with Chapter 2 and religiously do your daily self-help reading this way: spend one-half of your scheduled time reading *new* material and one-half of your time *rereading* the material you read the day before. Why? Because first readings only make people aware of what they need to learn. It's the second reading that starts their learning process.

When you complete a chapter, freely use the answers to the memory-aid questions for answering them. The questions are not to test you; they are to reinforce your long-term memory. The pages where the correct answers appear are listed at the end of the questions.

All of the chapters follow a logical sequence; each one prepares you for the next one. If you read them in numbered order, they will give you the best results.

What if some days you want to do more than an hour of self-help reading? By all means spend that time reading this book; but do *not* read new material. Instead, spend that extra time reviewing any notes you have made and the chapters you have already read. Also mentally review how you have already been applying your new ideas in your life. Or vividly imagine how you could have and/or how you immediately shall start applying it. Such use of your extra time will be much more helpful to you than any new reading you might have done on that day.

During your undistracted moments between your daily self-help readings, rethink the instantly helpful insights you will have read. Then take and retake your behavioral prescriptions as often as possible. You can *not* OD (overdose) on them. And, the more often you take them, the faster they will help you cope better with everything in your life.

You may now be thinking: That sounds a little like work. You're right; it is a little like work. But remember, a little work is the only way anyone can learn anything that's worthwhile. And what could be more worthwhile than learning how to cope better with your life as rapidly as possible? Probably not anything. However, you can always get trouble quickly and easily, often with little or no work at all. But then again, trouble is usually the only thing people can get that way.

Memory Aid Questions for Chapter 1

1. Self-help books and novels are best read in the same way. True or False?
2. It is unsafe for you to try to counsel yourself. True or False?
3. People cannot avoid counseling themselves, not even by following the advice of a paid professional. True or False?
4. Self-counseling is (*a*) _____ ideas that you believe and then (*b*) _____ , to those ideas in logical, (*c*) _____ , and (*d*) _____ ways.
5. Item #4 explains why (*a*) _____ counseling is the only kind that controls sane, healthy people's (*b*) _____ .
6. How do you make an idea yours? By seriously (*a*) _____ it and then (*b*) _____ logically to it.
7. Recite the Five Rational Questions for Rational Self-Counseling.
8. The five questions in item #7 actually are the five questions for ideal _____ and emotional health.
9. Many common words often have both an objective meaning and a socially approved but irrationally subjective meaning. True or False?
10. It doesn't really matter how you read this book, as long as you read it. True or False?

11. What's the most common mistake readers of self-help books make?
12. This book is meant to be both pleasant and informative reading. True or False?
13. If you follow the suggested instructions, you will not only read each chapter carefully, you will (*a*) _____ notes, and (*b*) _____ your notes daily.
14. If you are like most readers, you will soon discover that you already know but have been ignoring many of the instantly helpful facts about healthy human behavior this book describes. True or False?
15. _____ really is the only thing people usually get quickly and easily the very first time they try it.

Answers appear in Appendix II.

CHAPTER 2

Your Instantly Helpful Self-Analysis

Instantly Helpful Insights

Most people analyze themselves many times every day. Every sincere statement they make about themselves is a self-analysis. Unfortunately, the self-analyses unhappy people make are often too self-justifying or too painfully self-defeating to be helpful. Maybe this is why the self-analyses you have been making have not produced the self-improvements you want.

This chapter describes YUPI (Your Unhappiness Potential Inventory). YUPI is a clinically proven, fast, safe, self-scored personality inventory. If you complete it honestly, you will see instantly how you may be unwittingly keeping yourself from coping better with yourself and your life.

Your Unhappiness Potential Inventory

This is a two-part self-checklist of common personal causes of unhappiness and poor coping. These YUPI items are socially accepted but inaccurate perceptions and irrational beliefs. Yet most sane, intelligent people in Western societies automatically learn them as they grow up. My emotional self-help research has clearly shown that when people honestly replace inaccurate perceptions and irrational beliefs with objectively accurate perceptions and rational beliefs, three things immediately happen: (1) their personalities improve; (2) their natural (i.e., drug-free) happiness increases; and (3) most important, their ability to cope better with themselves and anything else increases.

Why do sane, intelligent people learn the YUPI items? Every society has its general body of so-called common sense ideas about how people "should" and "have to" behave. Most of those ideas are basic facts and valid principles of healthy, happy living. But some of those ideas are merely irrational beliefs, based on our forefathers' and mothers' ignorance. Yet each generation keeps on teaching these irrational beliefs to the next. Why? For three main reasons:

First, all people are born completely ignorant of themselves and the outside world.

Second, when people, especially children, have no contrary beliefs, they accept as obvious facts the ideas that most members of their group—especially the adult members—accept and react to without question.

Third, most people *never* systematically check and objectively decide which of their "common sense" ideas are facts and which are foolish fancy. Instead, most people blindly pursue life, guided by three logical-sounding but incorrect deductions from these personal observations: The first is: "I have thought and reacted the way I do for as long as I can remember." The second is: "Most of the sane, intelligent people I know think and react pretty much as I do." The third is: "Since my ideas and behaviors are just as normal and natural as everybody else's, if I change them I'll be abnormal and unnatural. But I don't want to be abnormal and unnatural."

The three incorrect deductions are:

1. "My way of thinking and reacting must be right and best, at least for me."
2. "Any problems that I may have, have to be caused by some other person or external life event."
3. "My problems must be caused by some defect in me as a human being, which keeps me from coping as well as other normal people cope."

Fortunately, here's one of the most instantly helpful facts this book will quickly help you rediscover: *The fact that your ideas and behaviors are normal and natural does not mean that they are good ideas and behaviors for you to have.*

Now, why did I say " . . . quickly help you *rediscover*"? This book describes basic facts about how healthy, undrugged human brains and bodies interact. You may not realize it now, but you already have seen evidence of these basic facts in yourself. You therefore will rediscover and recognize them as you read further.

It's reasonable for you now to think: "Well, if that's so, why aren't I already coping better?" Like most poorly coping people, either you ignore these basic facts or you do not think about them at the times you need to act on them. Both habits are common human traits.

For example, most cigarette smokers know that their normal and natural smoking behavior is unhealthy and self-defeating. When alcohol abusers are sober, they know that their normal and natural alcohol abuse is unhealthy and self-defeating. Most people who drive without their seat belts buckled know that their normal and natural no-seat-belt driving behavior is unsafe. But in all three cases, these sane, intelligent people either ignore the facts or they don't think about them at the times they need to act on them.

IMPORTANT FACTS TO REMEMBER

1. Some of your normal and natural perceptions, thoughts, and reactions may be unhealthy and self-defeating.

2. To benefit from this, or any self-help book, you must be willing to learn more effective coping behaviors that at first may seem abnormal or unnatural to you. Then you must practice the more effective coping behaviors until they become natural and normal for you.

Special Vocabulary for Chapter 2

Attitude. Any idea that you believe in so strongly that you no longer have to consciously think about it before you correctly react to it. An attitude triggers such an instant and automatic reaction to an external event that it may seem as if the external event (instead of your attitude) caused your reaction. You may even incorrectly believe that the external event, not your attitude, caused your reaction.*

Unhappiness potentials.   Any perception or belief or attitude that is a common cause of unhappiness and/or poor coping for sane, intelligent people.

Psychoemotional pollutant.   Any generally accepted, so-called common sense perception or belief that is also a common cause of clinical emotional distress and poor coping ability.

Important Questions Answered in Chapter 2

1. Where did YUPI (Your Unhappiness Potential Inventory) come from?
2. If everybody learns the YUPI items, why aren't we all equally unhappy?
3. How are YUPI items like pollutants in the air we breathe?
4. Why is a big YUPI score unimportant?
5. Why is it that you will not have to correct all of your highly scored YUPI items in order to learn to cope better with absolutely anything?
6. What are four personal advantages of knowing your YUPI scores?
7. Why are some YUPI items very similar to others?

How to Do Instant Self-Analysis

To begin, complete the following two-part questionnaire called YUPI (Your Unhappiness Potential Inventory). I collected the YUPI items during ten years of clinical research on techniques of emotional and behavioral self-help. My research subjects were sane, intelligent, but unhappy people. Their main problem: They never had learned the skill of how to cope better with themselves or their lives.

---

*Professionally trained readers may be interested in the clinical discussions about dealing therapeutically with unhealthy attitudes that are in my book *Rational Behavior Therapy* (Prentice-Hall, Inc., 1984). But for learning instantly helpful self-analysis and how to use it to cope better, the above definition gives you all the insight you now need about attitudes.

These subjects differed greatly in their income, IQ, and education; and they represented all the major racial, social, ethnic, and life-style groups in America. Yet the ones who learned to cope better all had one similar trait: They were willing to do more than just read about the basic facts of healthy brain-body interactions this book describes. They were willing to make those basic facts the basis for new habits of daily living.

Remember now, many of the basic facts "felt wrong" when these people first began acting on them. But these people either already knew or they quickly discovered that when facts conflict with well-learned personal beliefs or attitudes, the facts always "feel wrong" at first. For example:

At first, the facts about the world being round "felt wrong" even to highly educated people. So when some of the basic facts of healthy human behavior described in this book "feel wrong" to you, just ignore that feeling and continue to read with an open mind. Then you will quickly find obvious evidence that these facts are the ideal basis for coping better.

PART A OF YOUR UNHAPPINESS POTENTIAL INVENTORY (YUPI)

"Common Sense" Perceptions (CSP'S)

The following twenty-eight "common sense" perceptions are all common psychoemotional pollutants. Each statement has a scale of 0 to 5. Zero means: "Never, this item does not apply to me." Each of the other numbers corresponds to a word: 1 = Rarely, 2 = Sometimes, 3 = Frequently, 4 = Usually, and 5 = Always. Circle the digit that seems most accurate for how often you seem to make that perception, especially when you are in distress.

Sometimes a YUPI item will apply to only one person or situation in your life. On the blank line below each item, write in who that person is or what that situation is. Then score the item for that person or situation.

Don't skip any items and answer each as honestly as you can. Remember, on a self-administered, self-scored inventory, the only person you can fool is yourself. Your YUPI scores will be your guides for changing yourself from an unhappy, poorly coping person to the happy, better-coping person you want to be.

Granted, no two of your days are exactly alike; there also may be many fluctuations within a day; but use the preceding guides and make your most honest estimate of how often each item seems to be a factor in distress.

YUPI Part A (CSP'S)

Scoring: 0 = Never; 1 = Rarely; 2 = Sometimes; 3 = Frequently; 4 = Usually; 5 = Always.

1. The reflection of me that I see in the mirror is not the real me.   0   1   2   3   4   5

_____

2. I don't have enough self-confidence.   0   1   2   3   4   5

_____

3. I won't be able to accept myself until I get more self-confidence.

0 1 2 3 4 5

4. I am not as good a person as I can and should be.

0 1 2 3 4 5

5. My life is worthless and unproductive.

0 1 2 3 4 5

6. (*Choose as many as apply*)
I see myself as being too fat; too skinny; too tall; too short; not intelligent enough. (*List any other such negative self-perceptions that you make.*)

0 1 2 3 4 5

7. I am a phony.

0 1 2 3 4 5

8. People use me and that upsets me.

0 1 2 3 4 5

9. It makes me angry at myself when I don't live up to my proven potential.

0 1 2 3 4 5

10. It makes me feel just awful when people treat me unfairly or unjustly.

0 1 2 3 4 5

11. It upsets me very much when things that really matter to me don't go right.

0 1 2 3 4 5

12. No one cares enough about me emotionally.

0 1 2 3 4 5

13. The solution to most of my problems is for certain people to care enough about me to fulfill my emotional dependency needs.   0 1 2 3 4 5

14. I have tried to change myself, but I just can't do it.   0 1 2 3 4 5

15. I am just unlucky.   0 1 2 3 4 5

16. I have to stay somewhat tense until I do the important things that I have to do; otherwise, I forget to do them.   0 1 2 3 4 5

17. When I hurt other people emotionally, it (that fact) hurts me more than it hurts them.   0 1 2 3 4 5

18. If someone does me "wrong," I feel that I just have to get even.   0 1 2 3 4 5

19. I don't let little things bother me; but if someone keeps piling stuff on me that no one should stand for, I really flip my lid.   0 1 2 3 4 5

20. When two people really love each other, a good, let-it-all-hang-out, but fair lover's fight gives them good feelings of closeness.   0 1 2 3 4 5

21. The very time I decide to be carefree and loose, something bad always happens.

0 1 2 3 4 5

22. It's wrong to believe that I am the most important person in the world to me.

0 1 2 3 4 5

23. I can't concentrate the way I should.

0 1 2 3 4 5

24. The very time I decide to trust people, they always let me down.

0 1 2 3 4 5

25. The world is cold, cruel, and unfeeling.

0 1 2 3 4 5

26. Only really stupid people get used or have other people take advantage of them.

0 1 2 3 4 5

27. Some people are just plain worthless; or they are so despicable that they deserve to be hated, if not damned.

0 1 2 3 4 5

28. When people try to make rational sense of their emotions, they lose their creativity and become nonfeeling robots.

0 1 2 3 4 5

PART B OF YUPI

"Common Sense" Beliefs (CSB'S)

The following thirty-six "common sense" beliefs are widely held, common psychoemotional pollutants. But it may well be that you never actually think these ideas as they are expressed here. Even so, these ideas still may be your unspoken beliefs, i.e., your attitudes. If so, they still can cause you as severe personal problems as consciously spoken beliefs would cause you.

For example, many short people feel hurt when they hear other people joke about short people; yet these hurt short people often circle 0 or 1 for the "common sense" beliefs (CSB's) listed below. By reacting to jokes about short people with hurt feelings, these people react as if they believe in these CSB's or psychoemotional pollutants.

When people react emotionally as if they believe certain ideas, their reaction indicates that those ideas are their unspoken attitudes. Unspoken attitudes communicate the same behavioral messages as spoken beliefs communicate. The behavioral messages for the hurt short people mentioned above might be:

CSB #1: I believe that I should be different from the way I am.
CSB #29: I believe that if certain people were to treat me the way they should, I could feel better about myself and accept myself better.
CSB #30: I believe that if I could just make certain people see how their actions cause me such emotional pain, they would treat me better.

For such people to stop feeling hurt in response to jokes about short people they *must* discover, erase, and replace their unspoken (i.e., attitude) forms of the above beliefs. So, before you circle 0, 1, or 2 for a YUPI item, answer this question: "Do I react emotionally as if I believe that idea?" Then score the item, based on your honest answer to that question. Otherwise the instructions for taking and scoring Part B of YUPI are exactly the same as they were for Part A.

YUPI Part B (CSB'S)

Scoring: 0 = Never, this item does not apply to me; 1 = Rarely;
2 = Sometimes; 3 = Frequently; 4 = Usually; 5 = Always.

1. I believe that I ought to or should be
   different from the way I am: prettier,
   skinnier, taller, smarter, etc. Write in
   any other differences you believe
   apply to you.   0 1 2 3 4 5

   _____

2. I believe that I would like and accept
   myself better if I had more self-con-
   fidence.   0 1 2 3 4 5

   _____

3. I believe that I ought to be or should
   be a better person.   0 1 2 3 4 5

   _____

4. I believe all people should live lives
   that are generally considered to be
   worthwhile, productive lives.   0 1 2 3 4 5

   _____

5. I believe that if I act differently from
   my usual self, I will be a phony per-
   son, and I hate phonies.   0 1 2 3 4 5

   _____

6. I believe that a person's behavior
   shows what type of human being
   that person is.   0 1 2 3 4 5

   _____

7. I believe that I am a born worrier.   0 1 2 3 4 5

   _____

8. I believe that people should live up to
   their potential.   0 1 2 3 4 5

   _____

9. I believe there is me and another "real" me.

0 1 2 3 4 5

10. I believe my emotional feelings are more important than my thoughts in providing me with useful self-understanding and helpful insights.

0 1 2 3 4 5

11. I believe that people just have to be unhappy if there is no one around who really cares about them.

0 1 2 3 4 5

12. I believe that I am incapable of sexually satisfying members of the opposite sex and it depresses me.

0 1 2 3 4 5

13. I believe that people must have goals in their lives that are generally accepted as worthwhile before they can accept themselves.

0 1 2 3 4 5

14. I believe that if people get to know the real me, they will not like me, and that will be awful or terrible.

0 1 2 3 4 5

15. I believe that I can tell when people are thinking bad things about me, regardless of their attempts to deceive me.

0 1 2 3 4 5

16. I believe that what "feels right" to me is the most important thing for me to consider in deciding how it's best for me to think, act, and react.

0 1 2 3 4 5

17. I believe people should try to please other people, even if they are not pleased themselves.   0 1 2 3 4 5

18. I believe that it's my regrettable past that is causing my personal problems now.   0 1 2 3 4 5

19. I believe that worry sometimes helps me.   0 1 2 3 4 5

20. I believe that people (including myself) ought to be punished when they don't behave the way they should.   0 1 2 3 4 5

21. I believe it's natural and normal to be upset when things that are really important to me don't go the way they should.   0 1 2 3 4 5

22. I believe that people who control their emotions don't really enjoy life; they are like robots.   0 1 2 3 4 5

23. I believe people are happiest when their emotions are spontaneous, free, and uncontrolled.   0 1 2 3 4 5

24. I believe people have to feel guilty about their shortcomings and failures; otherwise, they are not normal people, but are psychopaths.   0 1 2 3 4 5

25. I believe that how badly I feel when a loved one leaves me, or otherwise behaves undesirably, shows how much I really care for that person.

    0   1   2   3   4   5

26. I believe that being really sincere in my desires and really honest about my emotions are the most important factors in making things turn out the way I want them to turn out.

    0   1   2   3   4   5

27. I believe that my usual emotional responses to people and life events are real, natural, and normal feelings for me, and I would not be the "real" me if I changed them.

    0   1   2   3   4   5

28. I believe that if I make an honest effort to do something and still fail at it, I can't do it, or it's just not meant for me to have that success.

    0   1   2   3   4   5

29. I believe that if certain people were to treat me the way they should, I could feel better about myself and accept myself better.

    0   1   2   3   4   5

30. I believe that if I could just make certain people see how their actions cause me such emotional pain, they would treat me better.

    0   1   2   3   4   5

31. I believe that people have to love themselves in order to accept themselves.

    0   1   2   3   4   5

32. I believe that there are universal standards of right and wrong that everyone should follow regardless of their personal feelings.

0 1 2 3 4 5

33. I believe that everyone needs to be loved in order to accept him or herself.

0 1 2 3 4 5

34. I believe that everyone ought to put other people's feelings ahead of their own more often.

0 1 2 3 4 5

35. I believe that how one person treats another person is the main factor in determining how that person feels about him or herself and whether or not that person has a positive self-image or positive self-acceptance.

0 1 2 3 4 5

36. I believe that magical powers are a factor in determining what happens in my life.

0 1 2 3 4 5

Now *please* forget about YUPI until you later reach Section V. Section V gives you the helpful facts and behavior prescriptions to use for the YUPI items that you scored higher than 2. By then (if you have read as suggested) you automatically will have reduced the negative influence many of your highly scored items have on you.

The Best Way to Think about YUPI Items

YUPI items are quite like the pollutants in the air we breathe. Not one of the pollutants is healthy for any of us. Fortunately, though, most of us have only average sensitivity to pollutants; also, most of the time the level of air pollution stays within an average range. That's why most of us can breathe our polluted air and still live reasonably comfortable, healthy lives.

But what about people who are hypersensitive and hyperreactive to common air pollutants? They often have unhealthy, sometimes even deadly reactions to average or even below-average levels of air pollution. On the other hand, if the levels of normal air pollution rise high enough, many of us will have significant health problems, and some of us may even die.

Inaccurate perceptions and irrational beliefs really are psychoemotional pollutants. That's why they affect people emotionally in much the same way that chemical pollutants affect them phys-

ically. The illustration below is an example of the unhealthy emotional stress psychoemotional pollutants cause those who have irrational beliefs about what it means to be a man.

It doesn't matter that you may know many happy, successful people who would have scored the same as you on the YUPI items. Remember the air pollutants and psychoemotional pollutants that are harmless for most people still can be poison for others. That's why it will be best for your natural happiness and coping ability for you to mentally erase and replace all of the YUPI items on which you scored higher than 2.

In later sections of this book you will find healthy replacements for each YUPI item. You'll also find the reasons I prescribe those healthy replacements. But you'll have to discover certain basic facts of healthy human behavior before you can successfully use the behavioral prescriptions. So please don't skip ahead.

Why do equally sane, intelligent people have unequal coping abilities?

There are several reasons. First, people vary greatly in how many YUPI items they have learned, how many contrary or competing perceptions, beliefs, and reactions they have learned, and how often their life events include the same YUPI items. For example, virtually everyone has negative beliefs about being rejected, especially in public. Just the thought of public rejection prevents some people from speaking up or asking a question, even in a class on how to get rid of the fear of rejection!

Salespeople dislike being rejected, too. Yet they expose themselves to it every day; the successful ones actually enjoy that exposure, but never the rejections. They have learned some of the same techniques of coping better that this book will teach you. That's why they can overcome their fear of rejection and happily get on with their lives.

Here are two other reasons equally sane, intelligent people have unequal coping abilities. They vary greatly in how strongly they believe in the same YUPI items and how often they act them out in their daily lives. The power YUPI items have on people varies directly with the strength of personal beliefs and the frequency of their daily use.

FOUR PERSONAL ADVANTAGES OF KNOWING YOUR YUPI SCORES

1. YUPI scores are the fastest, safest, and most psychologically reliable guides to instantly helpful self-help efforts.
2. YUPI scores are self-calculated, therefore they give you complete privacy.
3. Your YUPI scores also tell you exactly where in Section V to find the new, healthier ideas and behaviors that will instantly increase your natural happiness and your best coping skills.
4. Even if you are already as happy as you want to be, you probably still have YUPI items that qualify for being erased and replaced. Finding, erasing, and replacing these YUPI items will enable you to cope better with whatever awaits you tomorrow.

REPETITION AND DUPLICATION WITHIN YUPI

Many of the items in Part A and Part B of YUPI are similar, but no two are exactly the same. Cognitively speaking, there are two main groups of people. The first group consists of those who focus first on what they perceive or see mentally and only second on their moment-to-moment thoughts. I call these people image thinkers. Their brains work mainly like TV sets. They usually "see" a vivid mental image of most of the things they think about.

The second group is the concept thinkers. They *don't* usually see many vivid mental images of the things they think about. That's why concept thinkers see and describe the same life experience somewhat differently from the way image thinkers see and describe them. Concept thinkers' brains work mainly like radios.

Both image thinking and concept thinking are *entirely* normal, *healthy* ways to think. Everyone does both types of thinking. But certain people usually tend to do one type of thinking much more often than they do the other type. Because I can't know which type of thinker you are, I ask that you score every YUPI item as honestly as you can. If you do, your YUPI score may end up being surprisingly high. But please do *not* worry about that.

Having a high YUPI score does not mean that you are bad off, or that helping yourself will be difficult, or that it will take you a long time to do it. The YUPI items overlap and interlock in their influences on you. Therefore, when you start decreasing the influence one particular YUPI item has on you, you automatically will decrease the influence of the overlapping and interlocking ones. That's why it will be unnecessary for you to work directly on every highly scored item.

IMPORTANT FACTS TO REMEMBER

1. YUPI items are like air pollution. You can safely ignore some of them (the ones you honestly scored 1 or 2) most of the time.
2. Your total YUPI score has no direct relationship to how easily or quickly you will learn how to cope better with yourself and anything else.
3. To learn better coping skills, you will have to do mental practice daily and for a long enough time to make coping better your *new habit*.
4. At the appropriate time, this book will teach you the fastest and most effective way to do the mental and emotional practice you need to make coping better your *new daily habit*.

Memory Aid Questions for Chapter 2

1. Most people _____ themselves every day.
2. Every sincere statement about (a) _____ is a (b) _____ .
3. The self-analyses of most (a) _____ people are too (b) _____ or too (c) _____ to be helpful.
4. People's personalities have been shown to improve as they (a) _____ and (b) _____ inaccurate (c) _____ with accurate ones and erase and replace their (d) _____ beliefs and (e) _____ with (f) _____ ones.
5. Sane, intelligent people never learn stupid, idiotic, self-defeating beliefs. True or False?
6. If it's common sense then it must make good, i.e., healthy, sense. True or False?

7. Normal people (*a*) _____ if ever check the objective (*b*) _____ of their (*c*) _____ and (*d*) _____ or emotional (*e*) _____ .

8. Psychoemotional (*a*) _____ are generally accepted (*b*) _____ that cause unhealthy emotional (*c*) _____ .

9. Only people with low IQ's have high scores on YUPI. True or False?

10. Even if none of your YUPI scores are higher that 2, you are still causing your own emotional distress. True or False?

11. A YUPI score higher than 4 means that item is a sure cause of the emotional distress you are having now. True or False?

12. Two people can have the same YUPI scores and still not be equally emotionally miserable or happy. True or False?

13. Cognitively speaking, there are (*a*) _____ main groups of (*b*) _____ ; the (*c*) _____ thinkers and the (*d*) _____ thinkers.

14. Image thinkers have better brains than concept thinkers. True or False?

15. There are (*a*) _____ personal advantages to knowing your (*b*) _____ scores; name them.

Answers appear in Appendix II.

CHAPTER 3

Instant Stress Reduction

Instantly Helpful Insight

The ideal tranquilizer is the healthy, undrugged brain. When used in the rational way, such brains are faster, safer, and more reliable than drugs. That's because healthy, undrugged brains are examples of Mother Nature at her best, and science has not yet improved on Mother Nature at her best.

Next, I shall give you a behavioral prescription for instant stress reduction that enables people to make the best use of their healthy, undrugged brains. But that good result occurs only if you understand the prescription and take it exactly as directed.

The prescription is: Do the Instant Stress-Reducing Maneuver (ISRM) as often as you need it to keep yourself as calm as you want to be.

The ISRM is a simple breathing maneuver. Yet even when you are most upset, it will give you safe, quick, desirable control over your emotions. Then you will be free to cope better with yourself or anything else.

MAIN POINTS TO REMEMBER

The ISRM has two parts. The first part is a systematic breathing routine called the Instant Better Feeling Maneuver. Yes, it really does make you feel better in an instant.

The second part of the ISRM is the Universally Calming Perspective. This is a short series of objective facts that, if honestly accepted, will give you the most healthy, calming view of absolutely any situation in your life. Some people resist accepting this view of things at first. If you happen to be one of them, don't worry about it. Just use the Instant Better Feeling Maneuver alone. It will still give you much healthier "stress breaks" than cigarettes or coffee can give you. I recommend, therefore, that you give yourself an instant better feeling for at least one or two minutes of your regular rest breaks. If you do, you will have a naturally happier day every day.

Special Vocabulary for Chapter 3

Anger.   An urge to harm or destroy someone or something.
Anxiety.   Fear that does not have a specific object.
ASAP.   An acronym representing the words *as soon as possible.*
Emotive states.   Refers solely to the objective, and therefore measurable, internal physiologic changes associated with the various human emotions.
Natural happiness.   Pleasant states of healthy, emotional balance and inner peace, triggered *only* by rational, positive self-acceptance. It's the state of mind and body interactions that Mother Nature seems to have programmed all healthy human brains to produce automatically, as soon as people's objective survival and physical comfort needs have been met.

Important Questions Answered in Chapter 3

1. Why is the ISRM so rapidly effective?
2. What six advantages does the ISRM give you that a tranquilizer can't give you?
3. What is the most natural way to activate your healthy brain's pleasure centers?
4. Why do beginners resist smiling when they do the ISRM?

5. What are the three special things people normally have to smile about at all times and in any situation?

The Instant Stress-Reducing Maneuver

Monday morning at work, David's telephone rang. Before he could say "good morning," his supervisor's shrill voice crackled in his ear. Something was wrong with an important company project.

Though she didn't say it, David's past experience told him that his supervisor believed he had caused the problem and that he had damn well better get it fixed, like yesterday! In addition, she wanted him in her office in twenty minutes with his proposed solution.

David did not need a coffee break to keep him awake and keep his thinking straight that morning. Being the sane, intelligent FHB (fallible human being) that he was, his body instantly reacted with the most normal human responses to a hated, threatening situation: He immediately became angry and afraid. His adrenaline flow increased; his heart beat faster; his breathing rate increased; his muscles tensed; and his blood pressure shot up.

These instant fight/flight reactions are logical and healthy when people face a life-or-death crisis. The ability to have those instant reactions is what has enabled the human race to survive. Without that ability, our cave-dwelling ancestors could not have protected themselves against the ever-present life-threatening dangers of daily life. Most likely, the human race would have quickly died out.

We modern people still have the same type of brains and nervous systems as our cave-dwelling ancestors, and that's great! Our instant fight/flight reactions enable us to avoid tragedy when a speeding car suddenly swerves toward us, when our children tease a vicious dog, or when we suddenly face any of the real physical dangers of modern living. But David's sudden appointment with his supervisor was not a life-or-death event.

Most threatening situations in modern people's civilized lives are subjective threats. David's threat was typical of that rule. Therefore, he had no logical reason to fight or to take flight. That made David's intense emotional reactions both inappropriate and useless. Furthermore, such intense emotional reactions usually prevent people from coping best with their current situations. And that's not all; for people like David (who had already suffered a heart attack a few years back), sudden intense emotional distress can be fatal.

What if David had taken a tranquilizer? It wouldn't have helped him. Pills normally take at least twenty minutes just to get out of the stomach, and the tranquilizing effect comes even later. But David had to describe his proposed solution in twenty minutes; if he had to do that with a chemically tranquilized look, that probably would have been more harmful than helpful to him.

Fortunately, David had learned the ISRM in our stress management clinic. So he wisely invested the first five minutes of his preparation time in making himself stress-free naturally, with the healthy use of his undrugged brain. The pressure of having only twenty minutes to get prepared was significant. That's why David's ISRM was the best way he could have spent his first five minutes of preparation time.

First, David sat comfortably at his desk, closed his eyes, and put a warm, soft Mona Lisa–like smile on his face. That means he had just enough of a pleasant facial expression to cause his facial muscles to feel nicely relaxed.

Mona Lisa Type Smile

Then, he began pacing his breathing with these silent thoughts: "A, I'm breathing in." And as he slowly breathed out he thought: "B, I'm breathing out." Then, he always paused at the end of breathing out and thought: "C, I'm relaxing."

During that slow breathing experience, David kept a warm, soft smile on his face as he paced his slow, three-part breathing cycle with: "A, I'm breathing in; B, I'm breathing out; C, I'm relaxing." And he breathed mainly with his diaphragm so his stomach wall gently bulged out as he breathed in and gently flattened as he breathed out, but his chest hardly moved at all.

This is the *Instant Better Feeling Maneuver.* To get quickly relaxed, David vividly imagined how his body would feel if he already had achieved the complete relaxation that he was trying to achieve. Healthy human brains react to sincere imagination in the same way they react to objective reality. So by imagining how pleasant his relaxed body was going to feel, David was able to get relaxed in the shortest possible time.

Slow breathing breaks up intense fight/flight reactions within two to five minutes, making this maneuver essential for quick, natural relaxation. So practice taking four to five seconds to breathe in while thinking: "A, I'm breathing in." Then take approximately the same amount of time for thinking yourself through each of the other two parts of your breathing cycle. At that rate it will take twelve to fifteen seconds to complete a three-part breathing cycle. Breathing at this slow rate will make it physiologically impossible for you to stay undesirably upset about anything.

If you are a good visual thinker, mentally picture yourself in a relaxing situation. This is helpful, but not essential. Just silently thinking about a relaxing situation gives less talented visual thinkers the same relaxing results.

Unfortunately, threatening situations like the one David faced usually last longer than the two to five minutes it takes the breathing exercise to calm oneself down. So once you calm down, your next challenge is to avoid a relapse into emotional distress when you resume normal breathing.

To prevent this relapse you'll need a calming perspective that's appropriate for absolutely any situation. This is the Universally Calming Perspective. It will instantly convert the slow breathing routine into the Instant Stress-Reducing Maneuver (ISRM).

The Universally Calming Perspective

1. Even though this event is different from what I wanted to see,
2. until I can make it the way I want it to be,
3. I can keep myself pleasantly calm, naturally.
4. With a warm, soft smile on my face,
5. I shall continue to breathe at this slow, relaxing pace,
6. until I am as pleasantly calm, naturally,
7. as I think it's now best for me to be.

When you think the lines in the Universally Calming Perspective, replace the thought: "C, I'm relaxing" with one numbered line from the calming perspective; but only one line per breathing pause. Then your slow breathing pace will be: "A, I'm breathing in and, B, I'm breathing out," then pause as you think one numbered line from the Universally Calming Perspective.

Go back now and memorize the Universally Calming Perspective. Then you'll be immediately able to start using the ISRM today and every day.

The Universally Calming Perspective instantly helps you in two important ways: It reminds you that failure to get what you want does not require you to get undesirably upset. The Universally Calming Perspective also reminds you that remaining ideally calm is one of the most effective aids to coping better with anybody or anything at anytime.

As soon as David had established his slow breathing rate, he began to silently recite the Universally Calming Perspective, instead of: "C, I'm relaxing." And equally important, he kept his warm, soft smile on his face.

After just five minutes of the ISRM, David was as pleasantly calm as he wanted to be. He then used the remaining fifteen minutes before his appointment to prepare his analysis of the problem. At the first hint of rising anxiety, David would calmly slow his breathing and silently repeat all, or a part of, the Universally Calming Perspective.

It became immediately obvious to David's calm mind that no one person had caused the problem. In addition, David's cool-headed analysis pointed directly to the most effective solution. Consequently both he and his supervisor were pleased at the end of the meeting.

OBJECTIONS TO THE UNIVERSALLY CALMING PERSPECTIVE

Like many people, I, too, was initially reluctant to accept the Universally Calming Perspective of life. I was afraid this objective view of life would make me passively accept crime and injustice and lose interest in right versus wrong and in improving myself. But a little objective thought quickly showed me that those undesirable events just could not happen to sane, intelligent people. Instead, here's what the Universally Calming Perspective enables sane, intelligent people to do, in the most effective way: It enables them to pursue and change any undesirable things that they can and want to change. Equally as important, it enables them to stop getting emotionally distressed about the things that they cannot, or are unwilling to, change.

Still, the idea that it's best to smile and remain calm about the situations I would normally get upset about didn't feel right to me at first, and it probably won't feel right at first to you, either. But I urge you to ignore that "wrong" feeling, just as I did. New ideas *always* feel wrong at first, especially if they conflict with old personal beliefs. Remember, people just laughed when the first person said:

It took even the most well-educated people hundreds of years to start "feeling right" when they heard that idea. Like me (and most other intelligent people) those early doubters were impressed least by new facts that they were simply told about and were impressed most by new facts that they discovered for themselves. Unfortunately, only a few of those early doubters were in a position to readily discover the new facts about the shape of the earth.

You will not have the disadvantage with the new facts in this book. They are facts of normal human behavior that have been applying to you, me, and all other normal people since our births. So by merely reading on with an open mind, you can quickly discover or rediscover for yourself all of the basic facts you need to know to make coping better at anytime your *new daily habit*.

Before you combine the slow breathing exercise with the Universally Calming Perspective, practice rhythmically reciting the ABC breathing instructions within twelve to fifteen seconds. That's usually the best breathing rate for rapid relaxation for most people. Once you can breathe at that rate consistently, you easily will maintain your slow breathing pace as you alternate your "C, I'm relaxing" thoughts with the lines from the Universally Calming Perspective.

Stop reading now and spend a few minutes practicing the ISRM. First, use the ABC breathing routine alone. Then replace your "C, I'm relaxing" thoughts with one of the lines from the Universally Calming Perspective. Be sure to keep a warm, soft smile on your face as you maintain your slow breathing pace. Your warm, soft smile is the best natural stimulus for the pleasure centers in your healthy brain.

Pause here and practice for five minutes. If you are like most people, you were able to make yourself pleasantly calm in less than five minutes; but you probably weren't feeling particularly tense to begin with. This experience will be much more dramatic when you do the ISRM to control undesirable anger, anxiety, or worry.

If you did not feel more pleasantly calm during your first ISRM, don't worry about it. At first, people often need ten or even fifteen minutes before the ISRM becomes noticeably effective. Just be patient. Each time you practice, relaxing will occur more quickly and automatically. Soon you will begin to feel your muscles relaxing the moment you even think about the maneuver. In the meantime, remember that even it if now takes you ten or even fifteen minutes to get pleasantly calm, that's still less time than it would take a tranquilizing pill to start getting out of your stomach.*

SIX ADVANTAGES THE ISRM GIVES YOU THAT TRANQUILIZERS CAN'T

1. *The ISRM is the fastest way possible to calm yourself.* It begins working instantly, and it can make you as calm as you want to be in two to five minutes.
2. *The ISRM is the safest way to calm yourself.* You can *not* OD (overdose) on it no matter how often or how long you do it.
3. *The ISRM can be safely mixed with alcohol.* That mix is not only safe, it usually decreases your urge to drink.
4. *The ISRM can be done any place, at any time with your eyes open* — when you are caught in traffic, on a scary airplane flight, in a tension-filled or boring conference, or in any other situations where you feel undesirably irritated, anxious, or otherwise upset.
5. *The ISRM will not dull your senses or decrease your reaction time.* Unlike alcohol or other tranquilizing drugs, therefore, the ISRM will never make you a hazard to yourself or others, on the highway, on your job, or in your home.
6. *the ISRM has direct long-term benefits for your health.* A distressed body uses excessive amounts of energy and is less able than an unstressed body to resist infections, cancer, and the simple wear and tear of normal living and aging.

Granted, you don't need to practice to get relaxed with a tranquilizing pill. But remember, trouble is the only thing you usually can depend on getting quickly without any practice. The benefits of worthwhile things usually require a little time and practice.

---

*There is an excellent commercially available cassette tape called *The Mind and Body Relaxation Tape*. It teaches you the ISRM as well as healthy attitudes that eliminate the habit of having undesirable anger, anxiety, and tension. You can get that valuable tape by sending $9.95 to RSA, Inc., Post Office Box 22146, Lexington, Kentucky 40522.

GOOD TIMES FOR DAILY ISRM

I especially like to do the ISRM three to five minutes before meals; it not only puts me in a pleasant mood for enjoying my meal, it decreases my tendency to overeat.* I also do three to five minutes of the ISRM in my office in the midmorning and midafternoon. I do it even when I don't feel particularly stressed.

The numerous subtle irritations in daily life have a cumulative effect that produces undesirable tension. People then are likely to react with inappropriate anger or anxiety about trivial events. One- or two-minute ISRM breaks throughout the day will give your nervous system helpful as well as pleasant time-outs. These time-outs will prevent tension build-up and help keep you naturally relaxed. Naturally relaxed people have increased resistance to both medical disorders and emotional distress.

IS IT NECESSARY TO SMILE WHEN YOU DO THE ISRM?

No. But a warm, soft smile is the most instantly pleasurable part of the maneuver. Your genuine smile stops your buildup of muscular tension faster than anything else. Scientists in the Fall 1983 issue of *Science* magazine reported the following evidence:

Angry facial expressions that research subjects put on solely upon request still caused objective, negative changes in the subjects' emotive states. And when those same research subjects put on requested pleasant facial expressions, their bodies reacted with objective, positive changes in their emotive states. Those scientific facts explain why your warm, soft smile greatly increases the effectiveness of your ISRM. So even if you don't feel like it, keep a warm, soft smile on your face. It will instantly start, plus help you complete, the most rapid healthy switch from emotional distress to pleasant relaxation.

WHY DO MOST BEGINNERS RESIST SMILING?

There are three common reasons. *First,* most beginners don't believe they have anything special to smile about, at least at that

*I used to be a binge eater.

moment. *Second*, they believe it looks silly to smile without having anything special to smile about. And *third*, they simply refuse to give themselves the self-image of looking silly, especially to themselves.

Fortunately, the research I have described proves that you (and everyone else) always have something special to smile about. What is it? It's the fact that your smiling face instantly triggers more pleasant bodily changes than your other facial expressions trigger.

You can easily prove this to yourself in thirty seconds. Put on and hold for ten seconds your most negative facial expression; then follow that facial expression with ten seconds of your most blank or poker-faced expression. Then follow that facial expression with ten seconds of your warm, soft Mona Lisa–like smiling expression. If you are like most people, your Mona Lisa–like smile felt better than the other two. These obvious facts about smiling bring me to your prescription for a happy day every day.

The prescription: Face each day with a warm, soft Mona Lisa–like smile and continue that smile throughout the day.

Your genuine Mona Lisa–like smile will help you see clearly that you are in charge of your body and your emotions. And when you look at others, broaden your smile; if you do, most people will smile back at you. Then you will have the most popular reason for smiling: to return the smiles of others. But even if no one returns your smile, one fact is clear: at any time or place, you always have something special to smile about—the instantly better emotional feeling your smile gives you.

IMPORTANT FACTS TO REMEMBER

1. The Instant Stress-Reducing Maneuver is faster, safer, and more reliable than alcohol, tranquilizers, or other drugs.
2. The most rapidly pleasant part of the ISRM is your warm, soft smile. It instantly triggers the internal bodily changes that produce naturally pleasant emotional states.
3. You can do the ISRM at any time or place that you want to feel better in the fastest and safest way possible.

Memory Aid Questions for Chapter 3

1. What is the purpose of memorizing and recalling the Universally Calming Perspective to your slow breathing exercise?
2. In the ISRM, you breathe using your (a) _____ and you keep a warm, soft (b) _____ on your face.
3. It's best to learn to recite the ABC slow breathing instructions in (a) _____ to (b) _____ seconds.
4. The ISRM has six advantages over tranquilizers. Name three.
5. What single act can stop the buildup of muscular tension faster than anything else?
6. Research has shown that natural smiling, but not smiles on the request of others, can cause the physiological responses that produce positive emotional states. True or False?
7. Give two good reasons you always have for smiling all day, every day.
8. What are two good times to do the ISRM?
9. What is one advantage that tranquilizers give people who have healthy brains that the ISRM can't give them?
10. It's absolutely essential to smile when doing the ISRM. True or False?

Answers appear in Appendix II.

SECTION II

Taking the "It-Monsters" out of Your Emotional Control

Congratulations for reading this far; you probably are serious about learning how to cope better with your life. Your best first step is to take the "It-Monsters" out of your emotional control forever.

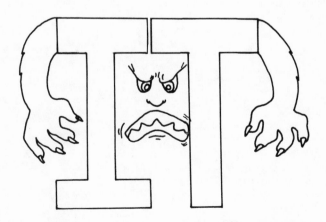

"It-Monsters" are all the nonphysical things people do that influence you, plus the nonphysical events in life that seem to upset you or otherwise control your emotions. Common descriptions are: "It upsets me, makes me mad, depresses me. She or he makes me feel good, turns me on, turns me off. It just drives me crazy, up the walls, insane," etc. This section shows you how and why you are always "It" and neither "she" nor "he" ever do anything to you emotionally.

CHAPTER 4

The A,B,C's of Normal Human Emotions

Instantly Helpful Insights

Thousands of people have consulted me to learn how to cope better with their lives. But only rarely have any come to my office complaining about how badly they have been thinking lately. Almost all have been complaining about how badly they have been feeling lately. In addition, they all have blamed their bad emotional feelings, at least in part, on the "It-Monsters," i.e., the undesirable external events and/or the other people in their lives.

With simply, everyday examples, this chapter gives you instantly helpful facts about how human emotions really work. Many of these facts are the opposite of what most people believe about how their emotions work. If you are one of those people, these facts will feel wrong to you at first. But don't worry about it. Instead, just calmly remember these two basic laws of Mother Nature:

1. New facts always feel wrong at first, if they conflict with old personal beliefs.
2. So far as scientists can now tell, the world was still round, even during the many centuries when it felt wrong to think so.

Fifty million Frenchmen (or any other people) can be and often are wrong (i.e., out of step with Mother Nature). And they are free to stay out of step for as long as they insist on it. Mother Nature is infinitely patient, but unforgiving. That's why people always get the most logical emotional and behavioral results for the ideas they believe and act out.

Special Vocabulary for Chapter 4

Belief. Any familiar idea to which people repeatedly respond with the same logical emotional feelings and/or physical reactions.
Believing. Thinking ideas and reacting to them with logical emotional and/or physical reactions.
Correct (as used in both Rational Behavior Therapy and in Rational Self-Counseling). A label for what most precisely describes the objective facts in any situation.* For example: "Two

---

* See Chapter 4 in *Rational Behavior Therapy* by Maxie C. Maultsby, Jr., M.D. (Prentice-Hall, Inc., 1984) for an excellent discussion of how your words control your emotional reactions.

plus two equals four" is correct. But what if I angrily believe that that fact should not be? Then my anger would be right (see definition of "right," below) for my belief, but wrong for the obvious facts.

Emotions. Inner urges to act in specific ways in specific situations; the urges consist of personal perceptions, beliefs, and attitudes, plus the logical emotional feelings triggered by those beliefs and attitudes.

Lie. Any idea the speakers do not believe but try to get others to believe is a fact.

Mind's eye. The part of people's minds that consists mainly of mental pictures, images, or impressions of objects or events that are triggered both by people's sincere words and the other stimuli for mentally picturing objects or events.

Perceptions. Any stimulus a person reacts to.

Right (from the practical, behavioral point of view as well as how it's used in Rational Behavior Therapy and Rational Self-Counseling). Whatever response two or more people agree to accept as appropriate for a given situation; or, whatever response the person in enforceable authority says is appropriate.

From an *emotional* point of view, however, right is whatever response that is most logical and appropriate for the belief or attitude that triggered it. That basic fact of normal human behavior was described over three thousand years ago with these words: "Every way of people is right in their own eyes" (*Proverbs* 21:2). In other words, merely by believing an idea, people make that idea right for their life experiences of that moment. But those ideas still can be incorrect for the facts and therefore contrary to what is best for those people.

Sincere thought. Any idea people react to with logical, emotional, and/or physical reactions. It's the most temporary form of a belief.

Subjective life experience. The sum of people's emotional and physical reactions to their beliefs about specific events. For example, if I believe that someone has cheated me out of one thousand dollars, even if my belief is incorrect, I will have the same subjective life experience (until I correct my belief) that I believe a cheated person should have. Under the influence of my incorrect belief, I would have the same anger, and call the police and do all the things I would do if I really had been cheated. In addition, my incorrect belief might cause me to overlook or ignore objective evidence that I had not been cheated. But relevant objective facts almost never will cause me to overlook or ignore correct beliefs. Those facts show that subjective life experiences (and not objective facts) are the most important psychological events in a person's life.

Important Questions Answered in Chapter 4

1. What are the A,B,C's of normal human emotions?
2. What's the important thing to remember about normal, healthy, and helpful behaviors?
3. What extremely helpful emotional fact does the A,B,C model of normal human emotions instantly make clear?
4. What's the basic difference between how physical feelings and how emotional feelings come about?
5. Which has the most direct control over people's emotions: the words people think and believe, or the external events people perceive with their eyes and other sensory organs?

The A,B,C's of Normal Human Emotions

A. Your perceptions
B. Your positive, negative, or neutral attitudes and beliefs about your perceptions at A
C. Your most logical or right emotional feeling for your attitudes and beliefs at B about what you perceive at A

Before you can have any emotional response, you must first become aware of something; that something is your perception, or the A in the A,B,C's of normal emotions.

Your brain registers your perceptions automatically. That's a major part of its role of keeping you alive and comfortable. Then equally as instantly and automatically your healthy brain uses your attitudes or personal beliefs to evaluate your A-perceptions. Without first evaluating your A-perceptions, your brain could not trigger your most logical reactions to them.

Healthy brains only produce one main evaluation at a time. That evaluation is either mainly positive, mainly negative, or mainly neutral for your A-perceptions. Your personal attitudes or beliefs, called B in the A,B,C's of normal emotions, are the mental units your brain uses to evaluate *all* of your A-perceptions.

Your attitudes and beliefs at B (about your perceptions at A) trigger your emotional feelings, or the C in the A,B,C's of normal emotions. If your attitudes and beliefs about your A-perceptions are mainly negative, your emotional feelings will have to be mainly negative. Mainly positive or mainly neutral attitudes and beliefs force your brain to create mainly positive or mainly neutral emotional feelings.

Your emotional A,B,C's make the next three helpful facts immediately clear. First, your emotional feelings are always real, logical, and right for what you believe about what you perceive.

For example, suppose that you look out and see rain; that will be A. And suppose you believe that rain on that particular day is a "terrible" event for you (i.e., it has "terrible" consequences for you). Your belief at B would force your healthy brain to give you real, logical, and right, "terrible" (i.e., intensely negative) emotional feelings about the rain and/or the day you perceive at A. Your "terrible" feelings would be C. If you did not feel those "terrible" emotions, it would mean that you either have *un*healthy brain and body interactions, or that you are joking or lying when you say: "It" (the rain) is "terrible" for you on that day.

THREE HELPFUL FACTS TO REMEMBER

1. You alone (with your belief) would have caused your "terrible" emotional feelings. "It," the rain, would only have caused wetness. It would have been magical thinking to say: "The rain

made me feel terrible." Neither rain nor any other "It-Monster" can control any human emotion. That's why "It," the outside world, never does anything to anyone emotionally. Instead, everyone always does every emotional thing to themselves about "It."

2. All you (and other sane, intelligent people) have to do to feel instantly better emotionally at C is to think better at B about what you perceive at A.

3. Thinking is the single most important act humans ever do.

AN INTERESTING IRONY

Most sane, intelligent people freely admit that thinking is the single most important act they do. Yet their thinking is usually the one personal act to which most people give the least amount of objective attention. Why? Probably because thinking is a brain activity. But most people rarely even think about their brains; and they almost never know how their brains really work. So let's take a few minutes now to let you rediscover a few helpful facts about how your brain works. I say "rediscover" because (like most people) you probably have already noticed and ignored these facts many times. If so, that's one of the main reasons you are not now coping better than you are.

How Healthy Brains Really Work

Imagine for a moment that you are visiting me at my childhood home in Florida. My home is on a beautiful little lake that even nonswimmers usually can't resist. On your first morning there, you get up before anyone else and you rush out for a refreshing swim. The water feels great, and you are enjoying how the sun warms you all over as you glide through the clear blue water. Emotionally you are in a pleasantly relaxed, naturally happy state.

Then you glance up and see me run out onto the boat dock, frantically waving and yelling. "Hey! Get out of there! There are alligators in this lake! Alligators! Do you hear me?"

What would you instantly see in your mind's eye? Right! You'd see alligators! And how would you instantly feel emotionally? If you are like me and most sane, intelligent people, you probably would feel instant panic and you would frantically swim back to the dock as quickly as possible. Those would be the most normal and healthy reactions for that situation.

Now let's see what the A,B,C model of normal human emotions says about who or what would have caused your panic and other behavior. The A-perceptions of your panic would have been my word *Alligators* and your mental picture of alligators. But you would not have seen any real alligators then, or before I had yelled to you. If you had seen any beforehand, you probably would not have still been in the lake when I ran out there. So where would your perceptions of alligators have come from? They would have come from your personal belief in my words that alligators were in the lake, plus your fearful attitude about that belief.

Granted, my words would have been the stimulus for your perceptions. But my words would have worked as that stimulus only because you would have believed in them. I'll talk more about that a little later. But now let's look at what your belief and three silent attitudes about it probably would have been. *Main belief:* "There are alligators in this lake." *Silent attitudes:* (1) "Alligators are dangerous"; (2) "Swimming in a lake with alligators is very dangerous"; (3) "I'm not stupid enough to knowingly do that dangerous thing."

Your emotional panic at C would have been real, logical, and right for your belief and attitudes about your situation at that moment. But to fully appreciate the essential role your belief would have played in your emotional control, consider the following possibilities.

Suppose that the night before your swim, my kindhearted mother had warned you that I liked to play that trick on my house guests.

And suppose she had assured you: "There never have been any alligators in that lake and there are no alligators in there now. We pay a man to treat the lake with chemicals that keep both alligators and fish away. And where there are no fish, there will be no alligators."

With that information, would you still have pictured alligators in your mind's eye and panicked when I ran out the next morning yelling about "alligators"? Probably not. You probably would have maintained your mental pictures of the beautiful lake and of me ranting and raving on the dock. Instead of panic, you probably would have felt self-satisfied humor toward me for my "silly" antic.

Why wouldn't you have then seen alligators when I yelled at you? Only because you would not have believed in my words. Instead you would have *chosen* to believe in my mother's words.

FOUR INSTANTLY HELPFUL FACTS ABOUT HOW HEALTHY BRAINS REALLY WORK

1. In addition to working like real cameras, healthy human brains also work like "word cameras." That means a healthy human brain converts a person's sincere labels into mental scenes of what those labels represent to the person.
2. The mental pictures triggered by people's sincere labels have more direct power and control over those people's emotional and physical reactions than their external perceptions have.
3. Healthy human brains convert into mental scenes only the labels those people believe in *at that moment.* That's why your personal beliefs (i.e., sincere labels) are the main keys to both your healthy and unhealthy emotional control.
4. Healthy human brains don't care whether people's sincere labels represent obvious facts or foolish fancy. Healthy human brains just instantly convert people's sincere labels into their mental scenes and subjective life experiences of that moment.

That is one of the most valuable self-help insights you can make. Why? Because your subjective life experiences of any moment are all you can meaningfully know about your life. For example, if you had believed in my words from the dock, what would have been your life experience of that moment? You would have had the subjective life experience of a swimmer in a lake with dangerous alligators, even though there were no alligators in the lake. But if you had believed my mother's words, you would have had the subjective life experience of a swimmer in a safe, alligator-free lake.

Still, there could have been three alligators speeding toward you at that very moment.

My mother might not have known these facts: The lake caretaker was a binge drinker; he was then on his latest three-week binge; both alligators and fish had already invaded the lake.

Remember, your brain doesn't care what idea you believe *and then perceive.* Your healthy brain will instantly convert into your subjective life experience of the moment any idea that you believe.

Your Subjective Realities Versus Objective Realities

At this point, some scientifically minded people will wonder: But how does Dr. Maultsby know it isn't the other way around? Maybe it's what people feel that makes them believe and think, using their particular words. After all, when the weather is hot, sane, intelligent people do not usually think that it's cold; they naturally think that it's hot.

Yes, I agree; that's exactly how *physical* feelings usually influence people's thoughts. But with your physical feelings there is almost always an objective cause-effect relationship between some objective stimulus for specific sensory nerve cells in your body and brain and the physical feelings you notice and label with words like "hot," "cold," "painful," "soothing," etc. Therefore your healthy physical feelings have to be right, logical, and correct for their associated stimuli. And, unlike emotional feelings, healthy physical feelings are usually independent of people's personal beliefs or attitudes about the objective stimuli for those feelings.

Remember, though, people differ in their inherited sensitivity and reactivity to stimuli. Therefore there are significant differences in what people perceive as hot, cold, painful, etc. Still, the same stimuli for physical feelings normally activate the same specific parts of the brain and produce the same physical feelings, which then lead to the same labels. But there are no such direct, unchanging relationships between external stimuli associated with emotional feelings and the resulting emotional feeling human brains produce. That's why it's helpful to remember that *physical feelings don't work like emotional feelings.*

Even babies who couldn't yet talk would have felt the same hot or burning feelings in their mouths that these people felt. In addition, even people who sincerely believed the cake was cool enough to eat would have felt that burning feeling.

In the above example, "It," the hot cake, did indeed cause all three people to have the same painfully hot perception at A in their mouths. So they all logically chose the same label, "hot," to describe their feeling. In addition, those people did not have the choice of having a cold feeling in response to that objectively hot cake. Mother Nature seems to have programmed healthy brains to automatically create hot physical feelings in response to hot stimuli.

There are, however, extremely rare but healthy people who have extremely high sensitivity and reactivity to their mental labels. These people can produce physical feelings at will in response to their mental labels. The book *The Mind of a Mnemonist*, by A.R. Luria, (Basic Books, 1968) presents an interesting, easy-to-read description of the scientific study of such a person. This man could simultaneously raise the measured temperature of one of his hands as he lowered the measured temperature of his other hand. How? Merely by thinking and mentally picturing one hand being in a hot oven and the other hand being on a block of ice. Such feats demonstrate why and how the psychoemotional pollutants in Chapter 2 can easily cause some people emotional problems as well as psychosomatic illnesses such as ulcers, hypertension, etc. Remember this when you start reading the behavioral prescriptions for coping better with absolutely anything.

To complete this discussion of your words in your emotional control, consider the next illustration.

In this example, one person had a negative emotional reaction, one had a neutral or calm emotional reaction, and one had a positive emotional reaction to the cake. Obviously, the cake by itself could not have caused those diverse emotional reactions. Each of the people chose his or her own emotional reactions with the sincere words each chose to think about the cake.

IMPORTANT FACTS TO REMEMBER

1. The choice of sincere words you use to think is the single most important factor in your emotional control.
2. You alone control the words you choose to use to think. That's why you can easily think yourself to as much natural happiness and coping power as you rationally desire.
3. Thinking better is the fastest, safest, and most reliable way to feel and cope better at any time.
4. People often perceive in their minds' eyes only what they

already believe exists. But if what they believe exists *doesn't*, then they deceive themselves.

That fourth fact has been known and ignored by poorly coping people for centuries; even the emotional self-help counselors in *Galatians* 6:3 described it with: "If people think themselves to be something when they are nothing, they deceiveth themselves." The next illustration is a commonplace example of that fact.

Linda, the woman in the illustration, is the suicidally depressed woman in the case history that will be presented in Chapter 7. She had tried to kill herself because she believed she was a mouse and didn't deserve to live. Because that was her conscious life experience at that moment, that's how she behaved.

Rational Self-Counseling quickly erased and replaced her irrational belief that she was a mouse with this rational belief: She was an FHB (fallible human being) who deserved to live. Rational Self-Counseling also cured her depression and enabled her to start coping better with herself and everything else. But that did *not* happen instantly. Her next step was to learn the rest of the emotional story that's told in Chapters 7 and 8.

Memory Aid Questions for Chapter 4

1. Other people and external life events (*a*) _____
   cause human emotions; instead people themselves create,
   (*b*) _____ , and eliminate their own emotional

feelings with their (c) _____ and
(d) _____ about other people and external life
events.

2. The sincere (a) _____ people use to think have
   more direct control over their emotions than the external
   reality they perceive with their (b) _____ and
   other sense organs.

3. The (a) _____ you feel at C in the A,B,C
   model of normal human emotions are always the most
   (b) _____ responses to B, the evaluation you
   will have made, based on your (c) _____ and
   attitudes about your (d) _____ at A.

4. In order to feel better emotionally, you need only to
   _____ better.

5. (a) _____ ing, rather than
   (b) _____ emotionally, is the single most
   important thing people do.

6. Almost all people get concerned about the way they have
   been _____ lately.

7. But people only rarely become concerned about the way
   they have been _____ lately.

8. Explain the difference between being correct and being right.

9. The emotional A,B,C's takes the (a) _____
   Monster (b) _____ out of objectively
   minded (c) _____
   emotional (d) _____ ing.

10. Write your emotional A,B,C's for one of your recent angry
    events, happy events, and neutral events.

11. Emotional feelings are always (a) _____ ,
    logical, and (b) _____ for people's
    (c) _____ but not necessarily for the
    (d) _____ facts.

12. It really doesn't matter what words you use to express
    yourself when you are trying to improve your emotional
    control. True or False?

13. You can improve your emotional control without alcohol
    or other drugs, even though you don't improve your
    semantics, i.e., your choice of words in thinking. True or
    False?

14. Which really controls your emotions: (*a*) what you believe *or* (*b*) the obvious facts, whether or not you believe them?
15. Healthy human brains work like (*a*) _____ cameras and also like (*b*) _____ cameras.

Answers appear in Appendix II.

CHAPTER 5

Your Attitudes and Your Emotions

Instantly Helpful Insights

If you are like most people, most of your emotional reactions just *seem* to happen automatically. You perceive some person, object, or event and instantly you have an emotional feeling. Usually you don't have time to think anything beforehand; and often, you will not even have *wanted* to have that emotional reaction.

Such experiences make it seem as if some external "emotional monster" called "It" really *does* cause those emotional reactions. Understandably, you (again like most people) often accuse imaginary "It-Monsters" of upsetting you, depressing you, making you feel good, etc. And equally understandably, you may initially resist giving up blaming your emotions, especially your self-defeatingly negative emotions, on the "It-Monsters." The handy-dandy "It-Monsters" make everything seem so obvious and easy to understand and accept. The only problem is, "It-Monsters" are merely socially approved, "common sense" nonsense. In addition, that nonsense confuses and prevents people from understanding themselves in the most useful and healthy ways.

Here's the good news. For people who think rationally, this chapter quickly kills the "It-Monster" myth once and for all. How? Simply by showing them this objective fact: People's personal attitudes, existing in their own superconscious minds, are their only "It-Monsters." *"It"* (the external world) *never does anything to anyone emotionally. Instead, everyone (with their attitudes and beliefs), always does every emotional thing to themselves about "it."* This chapter makes that fact clear.

Special Vocabulary for Chapter 5

Superconscious mind. The usually unnoticed, functional mental unit of the brain that houses the mental mechanisms for instant, automatic self-control. These mechanisms come into being after people have had enough mental practice in pairing the same or similar perceptions and sincere thoughts with the same logical, emotional and/or physical reactions to have those reactions without noticeable conscious thoughts. The most common example of those mental mechanisms is an attitude.

Truth. Any idea a person believes; merely believing any idea makes it both true for the believer and right for his or her life experience of the moment.

Important Questions Answered in Chapter 5

1. What actually causes the instant, automatic, gut reactions that people get before they have time to think anything, and which emotionally naive people blame on an "It-Monster"?
2. What are attitude-triggered emotional reactions and how are they related to "It-Monsters"?
3. What are the only three types of ideas that influence emotional feelings?
4. Are the A,B,C's of learning to type correctly the same as the A,B,C's of learning real, logical, and right emotional reactions?
5. How can ideas that are objectively incorrect still be right and true for you?
6. What are the core mental mechanisms of emotional and physical practice?
7. Why are people often unaware of what their attitudes are?
8. Would you ever accuse "It," a page of written words, of making a typist's fingers move instantly, automatically, and correctly in response to the sight of that page? If not, why not?
9. What are the four main roles attitudes have in self-control?
10. What are the three steps involved in practicing an emotion?
11. What is the main reason some people fail to improve their emotional control, even with professional help?
12. What's the main function of any habit?

13. What question do you need to answer to find out what your attitudes really are about some external person or situation?

EVELYN'S STORY

Use your imagination and put yourself in Evelyn's situation. She was peacefully watching television on the first night of a six-week visit in the home of a friend. The friend's kid brother slipped up behind Evelyn's chair and dropped a foot-long rubber alligator in her lap. What do you think Evelyn felt and did instantly, without taking time to think anything? Right!

The little boy thought Evelyn's blood-curdling scream and sudden jump were the funniest things imaginable. But the boy's mother and his sister almost had strokes.

Before learning their emotional A,B,C's, most people would accuse "It," the rubber alligator and/or the boy, of having frightened Evelyn. But let's use the A,B,C model of normal human emotions to see who or what really frightened Evelyn.

First, Evelyn saw (or more precisely, perceived) the alligator in her lap. That was A, her perception. Then Evelyn jumped up in panic at C, without taking time to think anything at B. So it couldn't have been her conscious thoughts at B that frightened her;

she didn't take the time for conscious thoughts. Does that prove that some "It-Monster" (in this case the rubber alligator and/or the boy) frightened Evelyn? Of course not. That idea is just another example of popular, socially accepted, "common sense" nonsense.

In reality, Evelyn frightened herself with her own fearful attitudes about alligators suddenly appearing in her lap. If you doubt that explanation, answer these questions. What if that rubber alligator had been a rubber doll? Or what if someone had told Evelyn beforehand that the boy planned to play that trick on her? What would Evelyn most probably have done in both cases? She probably would have calmly sat there and laughed, instead of jumping up in panic. That proves that neither the boy or the rubber alligator frightened Evelyn. She just had an attitude-triggered reaction.

Attitude-Triggered Emotions

Attitudes are the unspoken, superconscious forms of people's most powerful personal beliefs. These beliefs are so well learned that people don't need to consciously think them before having their most logical emotional and physical reactions for the attitude form of those beliefs. That's why and how attitude-triggered emotions occur instantly, like magic. People just perceive a well-learned external or mental stimulus, and their silent attitudes about that stimulus trigger the most logical and right emotional reactions for themselves, i.e., for those personal attitudes.

Attitude-triggered emotional reactions occur even when you don't want them. In fact, they often occur when you are trying to prevent their occurrence. That is the main basis of the lie detector test.

Statements such as It upsets me, It depressed me, It makes me angry, It makes me feel good, It turns me on, etc., are either:

1. jokes,
2. lies, or
3. sincere statements.

No other type of ideas influence emotional feelings. When the above ideas are jokes, the speakers feel positive emotions regardless of what they blame on "It." When those ideas are lies, the speakers usually feel different emotions from the ones they would feel if their ideas were true. And when those ideas are sincere, they reveal the speaker's belief in "It-Monsters." Such people naturally, but naively, react as if their "It-Monsters" were external realities.

In every case, however, "It" will be those people's own personal attitudes. The A,B,C's of habit learning make that clear. So let's take a careful look those A,B,C's right now.

SUMMARY OF THE A,B,C'S OF HABIT LEARNING

A. Your perceptions

B. Your sincere thoughts about A

C-1. Your correct or "right" emotional feelings, triggered by B about A*

C-2. Your correct or "right" physical actions, also triggered by B about A

People learn all their habits, *including their emotional habits,* according to that same A,B,C sequence. An objective look at any example of habit learning, therefore, will show you how all attitudes form and work. Let's look at how people learn to type correctly.

Most people understand what's involved in learning to type, even if they haven't yet learned how to do it. At appropriate places in the explanation, I shall make this important point: Evelyn used the same behavioral A,B,C's both to learn to type *and* to learn her fear of alligators.

*Those "right" emotional feelings are the feelings of "rightness" that people learn to get automatically, merely by repeating those A,B,C's enough to form a habitual reaction.

To learn to type correctly, Evelyn initially had to think herself through every individual step. She had to make A-perceptions and have B-thoughts such as : "J; that key is under my right index finger; so I press it down to type J." Then she had to react logically to her B-thoughts and press down her right index finger. That was C-2 in the A,B,C's of learning to type correctly.

C-2 caused the letter J to appear on her typing paper. C-1 was a combination of the feelings Evelyn's finger movements caused plus the real, logical, and "right" emotional feelings her positive attitude triggered about her correct typing thoughts at B and her correct C-2 physical typing actions.* Evelyn then had to repeat the same process for all of the typing keys—not just once, twice, or three times, but as many times as it took for her to learn to have the correct typing actions instantly and automatically, without needing to consciously think herself through the individual typing actions.

Repetition: The Royal Road to Rapid Learning

Plain old repetition alone carried Evelyn from the A,B,C's of beginning typing to the A-b, C's of her correct typing habits. I empha-

*Sincere thoughts trigger both physical reactions and emotional feelings. But when talking about the A,B,C's of complete emotions, it's customary to just write C for the emotional feelings at C. But when describing emotions plus their associated physical actions together, it's customary to label the emotional feelings C-1 and the physical actions C-2.

sized "plain old repetition alone" to call your attention to these three helpful emotional facts:

First, all practice is simply just plain old mental repetition of the A,B,C's of habit learning.

Second, emotional practice is just as essential for learning an emotional habit as physical practice is for learning a physical habit.

Third, failure to practice at all, or enough, is the main reason most people fail to improve their emotional control.

Evelyn now types instantly, automatically, and correctly. She doesn't need nor take time to think first about her individual typing motions before she makes them. But she can type that way now *only* because in the past she did enough correct typing practice to learn the correct typing attitude.

The simple act of repeatedly pairing the same A's with the same B's and C-1's and C-2's made Evelyn's correct typing behaviors habitual and therefore instant and automatic. That same mental process also correctly explains how and why people have the automatic emotional reactions they incorrectly blame on "It-Monsters."

Attitude-triggered reactions enable people to have correct emotional and/ or physical actions instantly and automatically, without first thinking their old B-thoughts.

From A,B,C to A-b, C Attitude-Controlled Habits

AT FIRST		LATER
A. Your perceptions.		A-b. Attitudes.
B. Your sincere thoughts about A.		Now, there are no more conscious thoughts at B.
C-1 Your "right" emotional reaction	After enough repeated pairings of A and B.	C-1. Your same "right" emotional reaction
C-2. Your "right" physical reaction		C-2. Your same "right" physical reaction

Figure 5–4. Attitude-triggered Typing

ATTITUDE-TRIGGERED REACTIONS

The seemingly small change from A,B to A-b is important in many ways. The capital A shows that the old external perceptions are now the most noticeable mental part of the behavioral event. The dash between the A and b in A-b attitudes shows that the now unspoken messages of the old B-thoughts have been mentally conditioned to the person's mental scenes of the old A-perceptions in the original A,B,C's. That gives unspoken attitudes the same behavioral triggering power that the original B-thoughts had.

Understandably, therefore, any real or imagined example of the old A-perceptions can instantly and automatically trigger the complete, correct A-b, C behavioral sequence.

A USEFUL FACT TO REMEMBER

People's personal attitudes cause them to skip their usual or old thoughts at B and still get their habitual reactions at C to their old perceptions at A.

A PLEASANT SELF-DISCOVERY

You have known this useful fact all along. Like most people, however, you have been ignoring it when you think about your emotions. But can you imagine yourself ever accusing "It," the pages Evelyn types, or "They," the alphabets she types at A, of making her fingers move at C? Probably not. Your longstanding correct insight into physical habit learning makes that accusation seem naive at best. Like most people, you comfortably accept this objective fact: Evelyn (with her typing attitude) makes her own fingers move, even though she doesn't think about her individual finger motions before she makes them.

By now, you are probably getting comfortable with the following facts: Outside people's imagination there is no "It-Monster" that can make their "guts" automatically move—that is, cause their automatic emotional feelings at C. Instead, with their attitudes, people make their own "guts" automatically move.

The Four Main Roles Attitudes Have in Self-Control

One, attitudes are essential for learning habits. Without attitudes, therefore, people would not be able to react instantly and correctly on external cues without first thinking about their reactions. That would be most undesirable.

What if Evelyn suddenly had to think each letter before she typed it? Her typing speed would instantly drop to her prelearning level and her typing errors also would increase.

Two, attitudes are essential for self-protection. Without attitudes many people would needlessly die or suffer physical harm. Imagine what would happen if auto drivers first had to think, "There is a person in front of my car. I had better step on my brakes," before they stopped their cars. Much more often than not, they would run over, hurt, or kill pedestrians.

Three, attitudes give people both their emotional spontaneity and emotional continuity. Attitudes are why people do not have to use the weather or the economy or some other "It-Monster" to help them decide whether or not to feel as loving today toward family and friends as they did yesterday. If people have loving attitudes, they can automatically feel loving regardless of the weather or the economy or any other outside stimulus.

Four, without attitudes, people could not improve their habitual self-control without drugs. Fortunately, attitudes *do* work the way this book says they work. That's why this book can teach you how to discover at will all of your self-defeating attitudes. And that's not all. This book can also show you *exactly how* to mentally erase and replace any self-defeating attitudes with attitudes that give you natural happiness, plus the ability to cope better with yourself and everything else.

Memory Aid Questions for Chapter 5

1. Most of your emotional reactions just (*a*) _____
   to happen (*b*) _____.
2. People's personal (*a*) _____, existing in their
   (*b*) _____ minds are their
   (*c*) _____ Monsters."
3. The three types of ideas that influence human behavior are
   (*a* _____, (*b*) _____ , and
   (*c*) _____ statements.
4. People learn to type according to the same
   (*a*) _____ sequence with which they learn their
   emotional (*b*) _____.
5. Practice is as (*a*) _____ for learning an
   emotional (*b*) _____ as it is for learning any
   (*c*) _____.
6. Only to the extent that your (*a*) _____
   personal attitudes fit the objective (*b*) _____ of
   your life can you cope (*c*) _____ with your
   (*d*) _____.

7. (a) _____ -triggered reactions enable people to
   (b) _____ instantly and
   (c) _____ without first
   (d) _____.
8. Outside your (a) _____ there are no
   (b)" _____ " that make you
   (c) _____ emotions against your will.
9. Attitudes are essential for (a) _____ habits and
   for (b) _____.
10. (a) _____ give people their
    (b) _____ and without attitudes people could
    not (c) _____ their emotional control.

Answers appear in Appendix II.

CHAPTER 6

Your Beliefs and Your Emotions

Instantly Helpful Insights

Many perfectly sane, intelligent people have undesirable (if not self-defeating) emotions—useless anxiety, depression, etc.—without perceiving any specific stimulus at A. They may wake up depressed or have nonspecific anxiety. What causes these emotions? People themselves cause them with their semipermanent mental units called personal beliefs. This chapter shows you how.

Important Questions Answered in Chapter 6

1. What is the main role beliefs have in self-control?
2. If it's sane and rational to be afraid of alligators, why was Evelyn's fear a problem?
3. What are the most important triggers for the scenes in people's minds' eyes?
4. Does it matter if your subjective life experience does not fit the objectively real world?
6. Which is more important for your emotional health, your subjective or objective life experiences?
7. Failure to do what is the main reason people who fail at self-help fail?
8. What's the best way to discover which old and now forgotten beliefs are still controlling your emotions as your unspoken attitudes?

From A,B,C to a-B, C Belief-Controlled Habits

	AT FIRST		LATER
A.	Your perceptions		No external perceptions at A; just your imagination, or memory of them
B.	Your sincere thoughts about A	After enough repeated pairings of A and B	a-B. Belief (your old B-thoughts have now become mental habits.)
C-1	Your "right" emotional reaction		C-1 Your same "right" emotional reaction
C-2	Your "right" physical reaction		C-2 Your same "right" physical reaction

BELIEF-TRIGGERED REACTIONS

The small a in the a-B belief unit shows that the scenes in people's mind's eyes of the old A-perceptions have been conditioned to their old conscious thoughts at B about those A-perceptions. The capital B shows that people's old consciously spoken B-thoughts about their old A-perceptions are now the most noticeable part of the behavioral event.

Figure 6–1. Belief-triggered Typing

The Main Role Beliefs Have in Self-Control

Beliefs enable people to learn correct emotional and physical reactions to both real and imagined life events without the people ever having to have real-life learning experiences with those events. For example, Evelyn's fearful beliefs about alligators enabled her to learn her habitual fear of them, even though she had never seen a real one. Here's how that happened.

For as long as Evelyn could remember, whenever she had thought or heard anything about alligators, she peppered her thoughts with sincere but fearfully negative labels. Her fearfully negative labels always triggered in her mind's eye dreaded negative mental pictures of alligators attacking her, plus at least a smidgen of anxiety. That mental process is emotive imagery. Regardless of their reason or intention, every time people repeat such a mental process, they are doing emotional practice.

Figure 6–2. Practicing an Emotion Mentally

After enough such repetitions, Evelyn's healthy brain automatically converted her dreaded imaginary perceptions of alligators and her sincere negative thoughts about them into her fearfully negative attitudes about them.

Please do not misunderstand me. I am *not* saying that people should not be afraid of alligators. Alligators are dangerous. It is both rational and sane, therefore, for people to be afraid of them. Still, it's also a fact that people can and do learn self-defeating emotional habits merely by doing a-B, C–type mental practice, using sincere but inappropriate thoughts and mental images.

The alligator story makes the next four facts clear:

1. People's beliefs are the most important cues for the scenes in their minds' eyes.
2. The scenes in people's minds' eyes have the direct controlling influence on people's emotional and physical reactions. That makes people's beliefs, and therefore, their attitudes, the main factors in producing their subjective life experiences.
3. Only to the extent that people's subjective life experience accurately fit the objective realities in their lives can they rationally hope to cope better with themselves or anything.
4. Personal beliefs (and not facts) are the main factors in people's subjective life experiences.

The Direct Relationship between Your Beliefs and Attitudes

Beliefs and attitudes both come from the same practice activity. Practice means repeatedly pairing (at least in your mind) the same perceptions at A with the same sincere thoughts at B and the same emotional feelings and physical actions at C.

After enough practice, your brain automatically converts your repeatedly paired perceptions and thoughts into nonverbal attitudes and verbal beliefs about the learning experience. This makes attitudes the unspoken or superconscious form of beliefs, and beliefs the spoken or conscious form of attitudes. In short, beliefs and attitudes are just different forms of the mental consequences of mentally repeating any new reactions enough times to make them habitual reactions.

Attitude-triggered emotions are the ones most people blame on imaginary "It-Monsters." If people want to get rid of their undesirable attitude-triggered emotions, therefore, they must: (1) Stop blaming "It"; (2) discover what their undesirable attitudes are; (3) and then replace their undesirable attitudes with more desirable ones.

An Important Insight

People can not just get rid of an undesirable attitude; they always have to replace it with a new one.

Failure to replace their undesirable attitudes is one of the main reasons people fail to improve their emotional and behavioral control. Unfortunately, most poorly coping people neither know what their most undesirable attitudes are nor how to find out. Let's look now at a fast, safe, and reliable way to discover your undesirable as well as your desirable attitudes.

Remember, healthy brains produce attitudes by converting repeatedly paired A-perceptions and B-thoughts into semipermanent A-b mental units. Those A-b mental units then trigger the same emotional and physical reactions that the old B-thoughts used to trigger. So to discover your attitudes about any situation, person, or thing, just honestly answer this question: *By reacting the way I react, I am reacting as if I believe what ideas?*

Your honest answer will convert your silent, unnoticed attitudes about that situation, person, or thing into your conscious, easy-to-see, and *easy-to-replace* beliefs.* Next, check those beliefs with the Five Rational Questions. If those beliefs prove to be irrational, immediately replace them with sincere, rational thoughts. Then practice (i.e., act out) your sincere, new, rational thoughts until they erase your old unwanted attitudes and become your new attitudes.

Now, let's apply these insights to Evelyn's experience with the rubber alligator. By jumping up in panic, Evelyn reacted as if she believed: "That's a dangerous alligator! It might bite me and that would be awful!" Those were the belief forms of Evelyn's silent, fearful attitudes; they were also the "It-Monsters" that instantly and automatically triggered her panic reaction.

*Remember the example of the short person given in Chapter 2.

Objectively speaking, Evelyn's attitudes were quite rational for real alligators. Normally, therefore, Evelyn would not have wanted to erase and replace those attitudes. But in this case her attitudes created a problem.

For the next six weeks, Evelyn was going to live in that house with that little boy. The little boy was never penalized for his alligator trick. Within a week, therefore, Evelyn would have been a nervous wreck—unless, of course, she learned how to stop entertaining the boy with her panic responses.

To enjoy her visit Evelyn had to quickly convert her panic responses to calm indifference. That meant erasing and mentally replacing her fearful attitudes with sincere, rational thoughts and then converting them into her new attitudes. Such rational thoughts were: Only harmless rubber alligators will ever suddenly appear in my lap in this house. It's perfectly silly to be afraid of a rubber alligator. As long as I am in this house, therefore, I shall calmly ignore any alligators I see. That's the best way to retain my sanity; it's also the quickest way to get that little boy to lose interest in his trick.

Just thinking those sincere new rational thoughts once, or even three or four times, was not nearly enough self-help practice to solve Evelyn's problem. But after just three days of intense mental practice in believing and acting on those new rational thoughts,

Evelyn began to calmly ignore the alligator trick.* Predictably, the little boy began enjoying his trick less and less. By the end of five days, the little boy had virtually given up his alligator trick and was trying to get Evelyn to play Monopoly with him.

Evelyn rationally let the little boy win a lot of Monopoly games. But that was a small price to pay for a pleasant six-week visit with her friend.

IMPORTANT FACTS TO REMEMBER

1. Learning healthy emotional control is as easy as learning how to type.
2. The ideas that are real, right, and true for you can still be objectively incorrect for the world outside your mind.
3. You have to *start* thinking better and *keep on* doing it, in order to *keep on* feeling better without alcohol or other drugs.
4. Thinking better means recognizing and replacing with rational ideas all the irrational ideas you think, *every* time you think them. Anything less than that is like trying to bake a chocolate cake without using chocolate.
5. Once you understand and accept the above-described psychological facts about attitudes, you make it completely unnecessary to blame imaginary "It-Monsters" for any of your emotional feelings.
6. A,B,C–type mental practice is as essential for learning new emotional habits as it is for learning physical habits, such as correct typing.
7. To see the conscious belief forms of your attitudes, honestly answer this question: "By reacting the way I habitually react, I am reacting as if I believe what ideas?"
8. Your old personal attitudes will not just disappear simply because you convert them to their belief form and then decide that you don't want them anymore. Instead, your old attitudes will still hang on in your superconscious mind until you mentally erase and replace them with new attitudes.
9. To mentally erase and rationally replace irrational attitudes, you

---

*Such mental practice in believing and acting on new thoughts is Rational Emotive Imagery (REI). Chapter 8 teaches you how to do it. But you are not yet ready for REI. Please *do not* skip ahead. Intense mental practice means two to five minutes of REI every two to three hours.

must practice thinking and acting on your new rational thoughts until your brain converts them into your new rational attitudes.

Memory Aid Questions for Chapter 6

1. We learn emotional habits the same way we learn physical habits: by (a) _____ ; that means pairing the same sincere thoughts with the same emotional or physical (b) _____ .

2. In A-b atttitudes, the (a) _____ is the most noticeable mental part of the emotional event; the beliefs, represented by B, usually are (b) _____ and are then (c) _____ .

3. Your a-B beliefs can make you have strong emotional responses at C even if your old external _____ no longer exist.

4. (a) _____ , and not (b) _____ , are the major factors in what people experience and call reality.

5. Only to the extent that your personal (a) _____ accurately fit the objective (b) _____ of your life, can you live a (c) _____ life.

6. To quickly tell what your unspoken attitudes are, you need only to ask yourself what question?

7. (a) _____ -triggered emotions are what emotionally (b) _____ people usually blame on the (c) _____ .

8. (a) _____ is the royal road to rapid (b) _____ , be it (c) _____ or physical learning.

9. Learning to type follows the same (a) _____ model of (b) _____ that learning all (c) _____ or _____ habits follow.

10. Attitudes are the (spoken or unspoken) form of beliefs? Circle one.

Answers appear in Appendix II.

CHAPTER 7

A Camera Check of Your Perceptions

Instantly Helpful Insights

Your perceptions are only mental pictures formed in your brain from both your sensory organ input and from your sincere words. The alligator story showed you that perceptions triggered by words have the most powerful control over human emotional and physical reactions. Therefore, both your emotional health and coping ability are limited by how accurately your words fit the objective realities in your life.

Often people's words reflect more what they "feel" the reality might be, rather than what the reality objectively is. That is a major cause of emotional distress and poor coping ability. That's why it's helpful to have a quick, yet reliable, way of making sure that what you perceive is objectively real. Probably the best such way is doing the Camera Check of Perceptions.

Special Vocabulary for Chapter 7

Mental impression.   Awareness of reality that is more nonvisual than visual.

Objective reality or fact.   Any object or event that can be demonstrated to exist independently of any one person's belief in or perception of its existence.

Important Questions Answered in Chapter 7

1. What is the worst kind of personal problem to try to solve?
2. How can you instantly, yet accurately, check your sincere subjective perceptions against objective reality?
3. What are two widely popular but emotionally distressing names that don't refer to objective things?
4. What's the best way to protect yourself from having self-defeating illusions?
5. What's the fastest, safest, and most reliable way to clear up self-defeating illusions?

What the Camera Check of Perceptions Means

The Camera Check of Perceptions means making sure that your perceptions are as accurate as the pictures of a video camera would be. If your perceptions do not duplicate the pictures a video camera would take, very often your emotional control and coping ability will be poor.*

A CASE EXAMPLE

Linda, a sane, intelligent, twenty-six-year-old divorcee, had tried to kill herself the night before the following interview.

> ME: "Why did you think that suicide was the only solution to your problem? What could be that terrible about your life?"
> LINDA: "I'm such a mouse."
> ME: "A mouse? Is that a fact?"
> LINDA: "Yeah, I'm just a disgusting, gutless mouse, and I shouldn't be that way. It's just awful; I can't stand it anymore; that's why I did it."

Author's Note: Obviously Linda was not a real mouse. But sincere contrary thoughts force healthy human brains to ignore obvious facts. Those brains then give people the mental pictures or impressions of whatever their sincere labels represent to them. Those

---

*I say video camera to emphasize the importance of making sure that you actually hear what people say.

scenes then cause healthy brains to trigger the most logical emotional and physical reactions for that person's attitudes or beliefs about those scenes.

That's how and why Linda unwittingly played the same emotional trick on herself that I played on my house guests in Chapter 4. My house guests believed my lie about alligators. They therefore reacted the way they believed they should react to the perception their belief triggered. That's all sane, intelligent people can do. That fact best explains Linda's behavior. She believed her lie about being a mouse. She therefore reacted the way she believed she should react to the perception her belief triggered.

Those insights about healthy human brains made it clear to me that Linda would remain suicidally depressed as long as:

1. She ignored the obvious fact that she was not a mouse.
2. She believed disgusting, gutless mice should be killed.

Now, what's the fastest, safest, and most reliable way to help people like Linda? In my experience, it is to get them to do the Camera Check of Perceptions. Sane, intelligent people will not continually ignore obvious, objective facts, even when those facts contradict their sincere word-pictures. But emotionally distressed people rarely focus on the most relevant obvious facts of their situation. That's usually the *main reason* they become distressed in the first place. Even the healthiest human brains can't react to facts that are not in their focus.

How to Do the Camera Check of Perceptions

To do the Camera Check of Perceptions, just honestly answer this question: Would a video camera's tape of your perceptions show what you believe are or were the obvious facts? If your objective answer is yes, then your perceptions probably will be objective. You can safely act on them as rationally as you can.

But what if your objective answer is no? Then immediately replace those scenes with the ones a video camera would have recorded. Otherwise, you probably won't cope best with that situation. Now let's get back to Linda.

This was Linda's first session with me. She had not yet learned about the Camera Check of Perceptions, so she had no reason to doubt the accuracy of her self-perception. That's why my simply telling her that I didn't think she was a mouse would have been a waste of breath. Like all normal people, Linda controlled her emotions solely with her own beliefs, not those of other people.*

The next illustration shows the perceptive correction I hoped to get Linda to make, using the Camera Check of Perceptions.

In response to Linda's statement: "Yeah, I'm a disgusting, gutless mouse, that's why I did it," I said, "Well, if I were to take a picture of you and show it to my secretary, do you think she would say: 'Oh, what a cute little mouse!'?"

Linda thought for a moment, then said, "No. I haven't felt very attractive lately, but I don't think I look like a mouse."

Then I said, "Well, why do you call yourself something you don't look like?"

She thought for a longer minute, and answered, "Well, you see, I *feel* like a mouse."

I said, "What does a mouse feel like? And when was the last time you asked a mouse how it feels to be one?"

Author's Note: You, the reader, probably think that by that point in the interview, this sane, intelligent woman was willing to give up her obviously incorrect self-perception. After all, she had just admitted that she didn't look like a mouse.

*This discussion applies only to people whose sensory organs are functioning accurately.

But Linda was still focused on the scene in her mind's eye of her being a mouse. So her brain could not then react to the obvious facts about her. In addition, Linda was then under the influence of one of the strongest fears sane, intelligent people have: the fear of being proven wrong. So, rather than admitting the obvious—that she was not a mouse—she did what most sane, intelligent, but unhappy people usually do—she defended her obviously incorrect perceptions.

Defending their obviously incorrect perceptions is a popular way people naively try to prove their sanity and intelligence to themselves. You see, sane, intelligent, but unhappy people *incorrectly* believe that only crazy and/or stupid people get emotionally upset about obviously incorrect perceptions. To avoid the self-perception of being crazy or stupid, unhappy people stubbornly search for any shred of credible support for their obviously incorrect perceptions. Unfortunately, the act of attempting suicide greatly reinforces that normal but self-defeating human tendency. Let's look for a moment at why that seemingly puzzling fact is easy to understand.

Can you imagine yourself immediately agreeing that the self-perception that had just led you to try to kill yourself is clearly an absurd mistake? Probably not. Most sincere but nonpsychotic suicidal people can't either, not before they discover their mistake for themselves. Predictably, therefore, Linda was not yet ready to admit that her self-perception was inaccurate, if not obviously absurd. Instead, she tried the popular but irrational tactic of reasoning by inappropriate analogy.

She said, "You see, if you get after a mouse, it'll run. Well, that's what I do. If you get after me, I run."

But I then pointed out, "But if you get after an elephant it will run, too. Are you an elephant? And if you get after a lion, it'll run, too. Are you a lion?"

As you read on, notice how easily my gentle but persistent challenges, based on the concept of a Camera Check of Perceptions, helped Linda discover her mistake. Also notice that immediately after discovering her mistake, Linda instantly improved the accuracy of her thinking. And as is usually the case when people improve the accuracy of their thinking, Linda instantly started coping better with herself and everything else.

In response to my question "Are you a lion?" Linda said, "No, what I mean is, I'm so afraid of rejection that I don't stand up for myself. I can't say no to people. My relatives ask me to do all kinds of cruddy things for them and I just have to do them."

When I asked for examples of those "cruddy things," Linda explained: "You see, after my divorce I moved in with my mother and she treats me like a baby. None of my boyfriends suit her. She won't let me raise my little girl the way I want to. She threatens to take my little girl away from me if I go to nightclubs or do anything she doesn't approve of. She even controls my money. My relatives don't come visit me unless they want me to baby-sit for them or help them clean house or something like that. And I just can't say no."

Author's Note: This is a good place to review the first of three important insights about emotional self-help that Linda's case has illustrated so far. First, the worst kind of personal problem to try to solve is a problem you don't have.

Linda didn't have the problem of being a mouse. That's why she had failed to solve it. Unfortunately, by herself she didn't make that insight into the reason she had failed to solve that problem. So in her painful frustration, she decided that she already should have solved that problem, "like other normal people would have." And because she hadn't done that, she decided that she couldn't stand to live any longer. And for that belief to have personal meaning, she had to try to kill herself.

Those psychological facts illustrate the next important insight: No matter how unhealthy or otherwise inappropriate a person's behavior may be, that *behavior always makes logical sense in light of that person's beliefs.*

Why? Because the healthy brain *does not care what people believe.* Healthy brains just instantly convert into people's conscious life experience whatever beliefs those people happen to have at that moment. Therefore, unless people then think equally sincere, but more strongly believed, contrary thoughts, they will react physically in the most logical way for their conscious life experiences.

Most often emotionally distressed people incorrectly describe their conscious life experiences as emotional feelings. For example, the night before this interview, Linda believed that her fear of rejection proved that she was a disgusting, gutless mouse that deserved to be killed. So she mislabeled her real fear of rejection, "feeling" that she was a mouse. But that mislabeled fear was still a real emotional feeling; that's why Linda naively believed that her real but mislabeled feeling was proof that she really was a mouse. That's how she gave herself the conscious life experience of being a "disgusting, gutless mouse" that deserved to die. So she logically attempted suicide.

Now what's the key insight to make here? It is that Linda's attempted suicide was just as logical as my house guest's panic was. In both cases, the people reacted logically for the conscious life experiences they gave themselves at that moment.

Those are the objective reasons why it's best to remember these three facts:

1. Your brain doesn't care what irrational or rational idea you believe. But whatever idea you believe, your healthy brain will instantly convert it into your conscious life experience of the moment.
2. To change your conscious life experience without drugs or brain damage, you must change your belief.
3. Your conscious life experience is the only aspect of your life that you can always change for the better or worse. You need only change your beliefs.

A COMMON QUESTION

"But what about when people's emotions take over like they did with Linda that night? What happens to their thoughts then?" Correct answer: Emotions never take over. Both emotions and physical actions are always the result of people's strongest attitudes and most strongly believed thoughts of the moment. That's why people need to know and think in terms of their emotional A,B,C's. Their emotional A,B,C's make it obvious that they are always in control of themselves—poor control perhaps, but still their control always.

For example, most probably you have occasionally felt like hitting or, at least, telling off one or two people in authority; yet because you didn't want to cope with the probable negative consequences of such action, you actually treated those people with all the respect due anyone in their position. That fact proves that (like all people's) your moment-to-moment thoughts control both your emotional feelings and your physical actions, sometimes even in opposite directions. Understanding and remembering that fact makes it easier to recognize the following one:

> A subtle, but common cause of unhappiness and lousy coping is the widely popular habit of thinking words you don't really mean, and meaning words you don't actually think, but believing in all of those words at that moment.

Now let's see if that applied to Linda's case. She called herself a gutless mouse; but she didn't mean that. She meant that she was afraid to say no to certain people; yet she didn't *say* what she meant until I got her to improve her thinking. Her suicidal behavior, however, was good evidence that she believed every word in her original ideas, even though she didn't mean them.

The main function of the Camera Check of Perceptions is to get people to keep themselves thinking the words they really mean, and really meaning the words they actually think, and believing in them. That's an essential step in coping better with oneself and everything else.

As soon as I got Linda to start thinking the words she meant and meaning the words she thought, she saw and accepted these obvious facts: *(1)* She was not a gutless mouse, therefore her belief that a gutless mouse should be killed *did not apply* to her. *(2)* A gutless mouse is already dead; therefore, she could not kill one anyway. *(3)* There was *no sane* solution to her problem as she had first described it.

Now let's see how I used the concept of the Camera Check to get Linda to correct her second incorrect self-perception, that she could not say no to people. Notice how this exchange instantly got Linda to say more precisely what she meant, even though she had inaccurately perceived it.

ME: "What do you mean you can't say no? You just said it to me."

LINDA: "When?"

ME: "When you said 'I can't say no,' you said 'no.' Right?"

LINDA: "Yes, but I mean that I can't say no when I don't want to do something or when I disagree with something."

ME: "*But that is not a fact either.* Just a moment ago you disagreed with me and said: 'No, I don't think I look like a mouse.' If you don't believe me, I can rewind the tape recorder and let you hear yourself say no' to me. Do you want me to do that?"

Author's Note: When people have healthy, undrugged brains, their attitudes and sincere thoughts are the most powerful factors in both their emotional and physical control. But until people learn and apply their emotional A,B,C's in their everyday lives, what do they do, especially when they are emotionally upset? They focus so intensely on their emotional feelings that they often don't hear their own thoughts. That's why I routinely tape-record all of my counseling sessions for my patients to listen to later. Only then do they hear everything either I or they have said.

Before I began routinely recording my sessions, people like Linda often angrily denied having said what I had heard them say. In addition, they often incorrectly accused me of "not caring enough to even listen" to them. So as an accident of self-defense, I discovered that tape-recording their sessions is an excellent aid for helping people focus on the obvious facts of their distressing life events. After all, the first rule in both rational thinking and coping better is getting focused on obvious facts. Ironically, emotionally distressed people strongly believe in that rule. In addition, they are usually most confident of their clear focus on it. Yet, as Linda's case shows, obvious fact is the one thing emotionally distressed people often ignore the most.

Remember, now, this was Linda's first session with me. I had not had time to introduce her to the Five Rational Questions for Rational Self-Counseling. But if I had already introduced her to them, I would have turned the rules into rational questions; then I would have gotten her to answer them. Her answers would have instantly shown her that her belief that she could not say no was irrational.

I would have begun by saying: "Now, let's do a rational check of your belief that you can't say no. Rational Question #1 is: Is your belief based on obvious fact? Do the Camera Check of that perception. Would a videotape of our conversation show you saying no?

Linda would have said yes. Then I would have said: "So your idea is not based on obvious fact. Rational Question #2: Does your belief best help you protect your life and health?" Linda had used her belief that she was a mouse to justify trying to kill herself. So she would have answered no to Rational Question #2.

ME: "Rational Question #3 is: Does your belief best help you achieve your short-term and long-term goals?" Linda was then suicidally depressed, so she could have honestly and accurately answered yes to that question. But, Linda was suicidal only because she believed her other incorrect ideas about herself. The goals she most wanted to pursue were being naturally happy and coping better with herself and her life. Therefore, after Linda would have seen that her original belief could not pass the Camera Check, she would have answered no to Rational Question #3.

ME: "Rational Question #4 is: Does your belief best help you avoid your most unwanted conflict with others?" Usually, Linda compulsively complied with the requests of others in order to avoid unwanted conflict with them. So she might have answered yes to that question.

ME: "Rational Question #5 is: Does your belief best help you feel the emotions you want to feel without alcohol or other drugs?"

Linda was suicidally depressed, solely because of her incorrect belief. Since her depression was both unwanted and seemingly unbearable, she would have answered no.

When an idea deserves three or more honest _no_ answers to the Five Rational Questions, that idea is both irrational and unhealthy for that person. It's best, therefore, for the person to replace that idea immediately with a more rational one.

I would have pointed out those facts to Linda, and she probably would have said: "Yeah, I see what you mean." Then I would have said something like: "So you see, the idea that you are using to run your life with is _neither_ factual, _nor_ healthy, _nor_ rational."

But, as I said, Linda had never heard of the Five Rational Questions. So, why did I tell you what I would have done if she had known about them? I wanted you to see how _you_ can instantly start using the Camera Check and the Five Rational Questions to start instantly coping better.

Now let's get back to what I actually did with Linda. I took you away from the interview where I had said, "I can rewind the tape recorder and let you hear yourself say 'no' to me. Do you want me to do that?"

LINDA: "No, that's all right. I believe you."

ME: "Huh? What did you say?"

LINDA: "I said no, that's . . . (She smiled then.) Oh, I see. I said it again, didn't I?"

ME: "Yes, you sure did. That's why I record my sessions, so I can quickly prove to people like you that their biggest problem is thinking ideas that they don't mean, and meaning ideas that they don't think, but believing in every one of them. That's a very self-defeating thing to do to yourself; it causes you to try to solve problems that you don't even have. And I can assure you, that's the worst kind of problem to try to solve!"

LINDA: "I don't follow that: What problem don't I have that I've been trying to solve?"

ME: "You've been trying to solve the problem of being a living, disgusting, gutless mouse, right? You even tried the ultimate solution to that problem: You tried to kill yourself. But you already would be dead if you really were a gutless mouse. Right? But are you now and have you ever been a mouse, gutless or otherwise?"

LINDA: "Well, no, not if you put it like that."

ME: "See, you said no again. And I didn't put it any specific way; I just repeated what you told me, which we both agree now was not even what you meant. But you still believed in it enough to try to kill yourself about it. Right?"

LINDA: "Right."

Author's Note: When I asked Linda what she had gotten from the interview, she said: "I create my own problems, don't I?" I said, "Yes, but if you start learning the rational way to think, you will instantly start getting more of what you rationally want out of your life without creating problems for yourself."

LINDA: "I sure want to learn it, because I have got to have some changes in my life. I just can't go on like this."

ME: "All right, I see that our time is up for today. Can I trust you to go home and come back alive tomorrow?"

LINDA: "Yeah, you can trust me. As you said, a gutless mouse is already dead, so you can't kill it again, right?"

ME: "That's right. So instead of trying to kill yourself, I want you to read the first chapter in this illustrated booklet entitled *You and Your Emotions*."*

ANOTHER COMMON QUESTION

"Dr. Maultsby, are you saying that everything a camera can take a picture of is a fact?" No, no, no! And that is *not* the logic of the Camera Check of Perceptions. The logic of the Camera Check is: If a video camera could not have recorded an event the way you describe it, then that description is probably *more* of a description of your beliefs than of the obvious facts about your situation.

Yes, people have a right to their beliefs or opinions. Their opinions and beliefs are the most important factors in their self-control; they also make them the unique, interesting people they are. Yet people's sincere but irrational opinions often cause them to cope poorly and keep them from having natural happiness. Quickly erasing and replacing such irrational opinions and beliefs with more rational ones are the healthiest things those people can do.

IMPORTANT FACTS TO REMEMBER

1. Stubbornly clinging to objectively incorrect perceptions is a common way unhappy people unwittingly prevent themselves from coping better with themselves or anything else.
2. The Camera Check of Perceptions is a fast, safe, and reliable way for people to get themselves to correct their obviously incorrect perceptions.
3. Where healthy emotional and physical control is concerned, it's never just semantics, it's always all semantics. To cope better, therefore, always say what you mean and mean what you say.

Memory Aid Questions for Chapter 7

1. Your perception of what is *(a)* _____ to you exists only in your *(b)* _____.

*You and Your Emotions is the standard bibliotherapy (i.e., rational self-help reading) that rational behavior therapists prescribe (or at least strongly recommend) for all people receiving either individual or group psychotherapy. For more information please send a stamped, self-addressed envelope to me at The Rational Behavior Training Center, Annex 4, Chambers Building, 820 S. Limestone, Lexington, Kentucky 40536-0226.

2. What are your two main types of perceptions?
3. The Camera Check is a *(a)* _____,
   (b) _____, and *(c)* _____ way to
   make sure that your perceptions accurately fit the obvious
   (d) _____ of your situation.
4. Your brain does *(a)* _____ care what you
   (b) _____.
5. Your brain converts whatever you *(a)* _____ into
   your personal life *(b)* _____ of the moment.
6. Linda really was a mouse for not saying no. True or False?
7. Where your emotional control is concerned, it's
   (a) _____ just *(b)* _____; it's
   (c) _____ all *(d)* _____.
8. To do the Camera Check, what question must you answer?
9. Linda started to feel better as soon as she started
   _____ better.
10. Stubbornly clinging to objectively *(a)* _____
    perceptions is a *(b)* _____ way people
    unwittingly keep themselves *(c)* _____ ly
    miserable.
11. What are the Five Rational Questions?
12. Do you now understand how to do the Camera Check of
    Perceptions? Yes or No?
13. What would be a rational reason for you to refuse to start
    doing the Camera Check every time you are upset?
14. Would your answer to item #13 help you improve your best
    coping ability?
15. If your answer to #14 is no, would it be rational to act on
    that reason?

Answers appear in Appendix II.

SECTION III

The Process of Learning to Cope Better

CHAPTER 8: The Five Stages in Learning to Cope Better—This chapter will tell you how to avoid giving up on improving your coping ability.

CHAPTER 9: Mental Practice for Learning to Cope Better—This chapter describes the easiest and best practice technique for mentally and physically erasing and replacing poor habits of coping.

Only dead people do not cope at all. You are alive; therefore you are already coping with every phase of your life. You're probably not coping to your satisfaction all the time (that's why you are reading this book); but it's important to know that you are coping.

Before you can start learning to cope better, you must first mentally and physically erase your present poor habits of coping. That means never excusing your irrational behavior with: "I know this is irrational but . . . " or any variation of that irrational mental ploy.

It is *never* enough merely to recognize and admit that your reaction is irrational, and it is an egregious error to believe that mentally erasing a habit means just promising yourself: "I'm not going to react that way *ever* again."

Mentally erasing and replacing a habit requires you to denounce it always, without exception. Then you must *absolutely* refuse to think any of the ideas that justified and supported it. Only then will you complete the five-stage process of mentally erasing and replacing those habits with better ones.

Here are the four separate erasing and replacing actions:

1. Choose the desired new habit with which you want to replace the unwanted habit.
2. Think only your new ideas that justify and support your desired new habit.

3. Consciously act out your new ideas every time you would normally act out the beliefs or attitudes that supported your old unwanted habit.
4. Repeat actions 2 and 3 until reacting in your new desired way is habitual, i.e., instant and automatic, requiring little or no conscious thought.

CHAPTER 8

The Five Stages in Learning to Cope Better

Instantly Helpful Insights

Many people choose to ignore that learning to cope better is a process. These people are most likely to get confused and discouraged and give up without improving their coping ability. They also are most likely to give up when they are in the third stage—cognitive-emotive dissonance. That's most unfortunate; a celebration would be more logical than giving up. Cognitive-emotive dissonance means people are just a half-step away from their behavioral goal. Even worse, people who give up at this stage also reinforce the incorrect ideas that overpowering "It-Monsters" really do exist or that their failure to help themselves proves that *they* are hopelessly inferior people. This chapter will help you avoid these undesirable fates.

Special Vocabulary for Chapter 8

Cognitive-emotive dissonance.   The unavoidable third stage in all emotional and behavioral reeducation. It's when people begin to think and/or behave in their new personally chosen way, but they don't yet "feel right" doing it. Their new thoughts and actions (even the most rational ones) still "feel wrong," i.e., odd or strange. That's logical; those new ideas and actions are then in conflict with the still unerased attitudes and beliefs that support the old behaviors.

Emotive imagery.   People having mental pictures or impressions in their minds' eyes of the scenes that their sincere words represent to them, plus the real or imagined emotional feelings that are most logical and right for those mental pictures. Synonym: mental rehearsal.*

Emotional insight.   The fourth stage of all emotional and behavioral reeducation. It's when people's new ideas trigger the new logical and right emotional feelings and physical actions for those new ideas.

Emotional (also behavioral) reeducation.   Mentally erasing and replacing one's emotional or behavioral habit with another one. (Learning to cope better is a good example.)

Intellectual insight.   The first stage in emotional and behavioral reeducation. It's having discovered what specific new perceptions and sincere thoughts people must practice to learn the new emotional and physical habits they want to make their new personality traits.

Personality trait.   A habitual reaction that people automatically have without needing to think about it beforehand. The formation of personality traits is the fifth stage of all emotional and behavioral reeducation.

Practice.   Repeatedly pairing the same A-perceptions with the same B-thoughts and C-1 emotional and C-2 physical reactions. It's the second stage of all emotional and behavioral reeducation.

Rational Emotive Imagery.   Emotive imagery that produces and maintains rational emotional and physical habits.

REI Scripts.   The rational ideas to be used to do REI—Rational Emotive Imagery. (The following chapters have all the REI scripts most people need to learn to cope better with themselves and everything else.)

Important Questions Answered in Chapter 8

1. Why is intellectual insight more important than emotional insight?

*When people (either naively or on purpose) use irrational ideas in their emotive imagery, they are doing Irrational Emotive Imagery. Irrational Emotive Imagery is the main way people unwittingly, but very effectively, practice and maintain their irrational emotional habits.

2. What's the evidence that you, the reader, probably already know about cognitive-emotive dissonance?
3. What real information do you get when an idea *feels* right or wrong?
4. Why do people get discouraged and want to give up even though they have almost solved their problems?
5. What's the best solution for item #4?

LINDA IN THE FIVE STAGES OF LEARNING TO COPE BETTER

Linda (the "mouse lady" in Chapter 7) was irrationally afraid of being rejected if she said no to certain people. Linda entered the *first stage—intellectual insight—*in learning how to cope better when she made these rational insights: "I can never be a mouse; so it's idiotic to ever call myself one; and it's even more idiotic to make myself feel as if I were one! I shall always be an FHB (fallible human being) just like everyone else. It would be crazy to hate myself about being that, or for any other reason. Like it or not, I'm all I've got, and I'm all I need to be naturally happy.* Hating myself only keeps me unhappy. So I shall immediately replace my self-hate with unconditional, rational self-acceptance.

"I can and will say no to anyone at any time I choose to do it. And I shall feel good about myself for doing it. If someone dislikes me because of that, then I'll rationally deal with their dislike as best I can. At worst, it will only be very inconvenient, but that's nothing to get suicidal or even very upset about."

Practice is the *second stage* in learning to cope better. The two kinds of practice are mental practice and real-life practice. Most people understand real-life practice and use it almost exclusively. That's usually all that's needed for learning physical skills. But for learning emotional skills, that approach alone almost always fails. Yet, like most unhappy people, that's the only approach Linda knew about.

LINDA: "What you are saying makes a lot of sense. And I'm going

---

*Natural happiness is unconditional happiness. It's a more basic form of happiness than the conditional happiness people experience in social and romantic situations.

to try it the very next time somebody asks me to do something that I don't want to do."

ME: "Try what?"

LINDA: "Saying no when I don't want to do something."

ME: "Good, but don't wait; if you wait, you won't have any more skill in coping with your fear of rejection the next time than you had last night. Start practicing and doing it today and every day."

LINDA: "But what if nobody asks me to do something? I can't just go around saying no to people if they haven't asked me something."

ME: "That's not what I'm suggesting. I'm suggesting that you do mental practice before you attempt your real-life action. Otherwise, what reason do you have to think that you will handle yourself any better the next time than you did the last time?"

LINDA: "Well, before I hadn't ever talked to a psychiatrist about it."

ME: "But there's no magic in having talked to me. I haven't told you anything that you didn't already know. Right? I mean, you already knew that you weren't really a mouse; and you already knew that you needed to start saying no when you didn't want to do something. Right?"

LINDA: "Yeah, I see what you mean. But I never felt like I could do it."

ME: "That's because you hadn't practiced doing it. So that's what we'll talk about next week, how to practice doing it beforehand. In the meantime, I want you to use the Instant Stress-Reducing Maneuver so you can start feeling better about yourself today, because you are not likely to start behaving better until you start feeling better about yourself. Right?"

LINDA (slowly): "I guess."

ME: "No, I don't want you to guess; I want you to know. So let's look at the facts. You have already made yourself feel badly enough to try to kill yourself. Right?"

LINDA: "Yeah, but if you feel good about being a mouse—I mean about what I'm doing, I might never stop."

ME: "But I'm not suggesting that you feel good about your undesirable behavior. I'm suggesting that you feel better about yourself as a person. You see, you have the same mistaken belief that most poorly coping and unhappy people have. You believe that people are their behavior. But people are not their behavior. People are responsible for their behavior because they do it; but they are not the same as their behavior; and that's why they can *stop* doing it as soon as they want to, *and* they learn how to stop doing it. You are punishing yourself for not doing something that you have not yet learned how to do. And if you don't stop punishing yourself by making yourself feel so bad, you will never get the chance to learn what you need to learn, to do what you want to do. Do you understand what I'm saying?"

LINDA: "I think so; but how do you learn how to feel better about yourself when you are a—I mean you can't do a simple thing like say: 'No, damn it, no'?"

ME: "Easily. Just practice. And it will be extremely easy in your case because you already know how to say no. You just need to learn how to start giving yourself rational self-acceptance so you can stop hurting so much, so you can relax and overcome your irrational fear of rejection, so you will say no when you want to."

LINDA: "But that sounds hard."

ME: "But it's so *easy* that in just one week, the page of cartoons about your emotional A,B,C's that my secretary is going to give you* and this mind-body relaxation tape that I'm going to lend you will teach you everything you need to know about self-acceptance. And then after your next appointment, we'll start using the tape to give you practice in calmly but firmly saying no at any time or place you want to say it. How about that?"

LINDA: "Fine, if you say so."

COGNITIVE-EMOTIVE DISSONANCE

Cognitive-emotive dissonance is when people sincerely *think* their new rational ideas, but those ideas *"feel* wrong" because they conflict with still unerased, contrary personal beliefs and attitudes. It's the unavoidable *third stage* in learning to cope better. Both mental and real-life practice force people to experience it.

---

*Upon your request with a stamped self-addressed envelope, as a public service the Director of The Rational Behavior Therapy Center of the College of medicine, University of Kentucky, Lexington, Kentucky 40536, will send you a free copy of his cartoon illustrations of the A,B,C's of healthy human emotions.

As long as Linda was in this stage of learning how to cope better, she still felt some of her old fear when she wanted to say no to certain people.

Her old fear made the idea of saying no feel wrong, i.e., seem like the wrong thing to do. But that was just an irrational illusion. Still, if I had not explained cognitive-emotive dissonance to linda before she experienced it, that irrational illusion would have confused her. Then she would have continued to say yes—which felt right but which she hated doing—when she really wanted to say no. Having learned about cognitive-emotive dissonance before she experienced it enabled linda to ignore her "wrong feelings" and say no anyway. Actually doing that was excellent real-life practice, and it quickly became Linda's desired habit.

GUT THINKING

Giving up or accepting a new idea (or behavior) solely on the basis of how it feels is "gut" thinking. Gut thinking stops people from learning anything new because gut logic is: "If it *feels* wrong (or if it does not feel right) then it *must be wrong* and should be ignored." That's why gut thinking gives people the Irrational Gooney Bird Syndrome, which causes them to give up their self-help efforts.

Figure 8–1. An Irrational Gooney Bird

Irrational Gooney Birds fly backward. They are much more interested in where they have been than in where they are going.

Gut thinking is based on attitude-triggered feelings. Attitudes are summaries of past experiences. That's why gut thinking only tells people where they have been experientially; and it keeps them there. But rational insight into cognitive-emotive dissonance will enable you to quickly overcome it and get on with learning to cope better.

AN EXPERIENCE IN REDISCOVERY

Like most people, you probably know much more about cognitive-emotive dissonance than you realize. This next example will tell you if that's so. If it is so, and you remember this example, you won't get confused when you experience cognitive-emotive dissonance while learning to cope better.

Imagine that you are a skilled American driver, but tomorrow you are expected to start driving an English car in England. In England they drive on the left-hand side of the street; therefore, drivers sit on the right side of English cars. How do you think you will feel sitting on the right side of a car, driving on the left side of the street in the busy London traffic?

That's a perfect example of cognitive-emotive dissonance. Your new ideas would be correct for the rational way to drive in England, but your still unerased American driving attitudes would be triggering your old, American-driving gut feelings. These contrary gut feelings would make you feel as if your new, correct English-driving ideas were really wrong and should be ignored in favor of your old American-driving attitudes and reactions. And gut thinking alone would cause you to do just that. But then you couldn't learn how to drive in England. That's exactly what gut thinking does: It causes you to do the very thing that you *don't* want to do and makes you feel right doing it.

In addition to already knowing those facts, you probably know this one, too: Successful English driving would require you to ignore your gut and do exclusive "brain thinking" as Mother Nature seems to have intended you to do anyway. Unfortunately, most unhappy people either don't know that fact, or they tend to ignore it when they try to improve their coping skills. The fact still remains, however, that to learn to cope better, people must favor their rational brain thinking over any contrary gut thinking. That logical act is the *main* key to success.

THE BEST SOLUTION TO COGNITIVE-EMOTIVE DISSONANCE

More intense REI and real-life practice is the fastest, safest, and easiest solution. It will quickly move you through cognitive-emotive dissonance into emotional insight.

Stage four of learning how to cope better, *emotional insight*, is when you have logical emotional feelings for your new rational ways of thinking. Your old undesirable reactions are rapidly disappearing; at the same time, your new rational beliefs and attitude-triggered reactions are becoming stronger and more instantly automatic.

Linda was in stage four of learning how to cope better when she could say no to anyone and remain calm, even though people became angry with her. Then, merely by continuing to do real-life practice, linda quickly and automatically moved into the *fifth stage* of learning how to cope better: *new personality trait formation*.

New personality trait formation is when people habitually have new, personally desirable emotional and physical reactions instantly and automatically. linda was well into this stage after three months of diligent real-life practice.

Memory Aid Questions for Chapter 8

1. What are the five stages in the process of learning to cope better?

   (1) _____   *(4)* _____

   (2) _____   *(5)* _____

   (3) _____

2. Those five stages do not occur in any specific order. True or False?

3. Cognitive-*(a)* _____ *dissonance is the*

   (b) _____ stage of learning to cope

   (c) _____.

4. *(a)* _____ -emotive dissonance is the stage of self-*(b)* _____ where people are most likely to get discouraged and *(c)* _____ up.

5. *(a)* _____ *-emotive(b)* _____ really means that people have *(c)* _____

   (d) _____ their problem.

6. Rational *(a)* _____ Imagery (REI) is the healthiest form of mental *(b)* _____.

7. The most effective REI is done using a written _____ script.

8. Emotional *(a)* _____ is the

   (b) _____ stage of self-improvement.

9. Most people know about and understand the cognitive-emotive dissonance of learning new driving habits. True or False?

10. More frequent *(a)* _____ and

    (b) _____ -life practice is the best solution to

    (c) _____ -emotive *(d)* _____.

Answers appear in Appendix II.

CHAPTER 9

Mental Practice for Learning to Cope Better

Instantly Helpful Insights

The basis for all learning is mental practice. The special mental practice technique used for learning to cope better is Rational Emotive Imagery (REI). REI has three essential steps: *(1)* sincerely thinking rational thoughts, plus *(2)* imagining the most logical mental pictures or impressions for those rational thoughts, plus *(3)* imagining yourself having the most logical emotional feelings and physical reactions for those rational thoughts.

As Evelyn's story (Chapter 5) clearly showed you, healthy human brains don't care; they work the same way when people learn either rational or irrational habits. That's why REI is all you need to do to learn to cope better with anything at anytime.

Important Questions Answered in Chapter 9

1. Does it make sense to try to practice an emotional feeling?
2. How do people practice their unwanted emotions without knowing that is what they are doing?
3. What were three common mistakes Albert made when he first tried to do REI?
4. How is practicing like pretending?
5. What is the main distinguishing feature of just pretending to improve one's self-control, as opposed to practicing improved self-control?

6. What is an example of sane, intelligent people trying to trick themselves into feeling better without thinking better?
7. What beliefs control people's reactions when they are just pretending to replace an old emotional reaction with a new one?
8. Why do people confuse pretending to improve their emotional control with practicing improved emotional control?
9. What are the three essential steps in doing REI?

ALBERT'S STORY

Albert (the subject of the case history that follows) cured his flying phobia in three weeks with REI. But he first had to discover how he was naively practicing and maintaining his phobia and stop doing that. Only then could he quickly erase and replace his flying phobia with the pleasant freedom to fly.

The illustration above is an excellent example of how Albert was naively practicing and maintaining his phobia. He was doing irrational emotive imagery; whenever he seriously thought about taking a flight, he fearfully pictured his plane crashing. That was the mental habit he had to begin erasing and replacing before he could start flying calmly.

After two rational behavior therapy sessions, Albert had learned the A,B,C's of his flying phobia and the Five Rational Questions. So I asked him to write an REI script for calmly making airline reservations and taking his first flight. In addition, he was to use his REI script to do daily REI.

A COMMON EVENT

Like many phobic people, Albert acted as if he believed this magical idea: merely knowing about writing REI scripts and knowing about doing daily REI should give him the same results as actually *doing* them. So, Albert did not write a REI script. Instead, he immediately began doing *his* version of REI. In effect, Albert was trying to bake a chocolate cake without using chocolate. Predictably, he got the most logical results for what he did. At his next appointment, therefore, Albert was still as phobic as ever and a bit irritated with me because of it.

At Albert's next therapy session he said: "I tried your REI, Doc, and it didn't work. So maybe we should try something else, huh?"

I have never seen a single instance where correctly done REI "didn't work." So I calmly pointed out to Albert that it had not been *my* REI; it had been his. I also pointed out that "trying" alone is the proven formula of failures. Then I asked him to tell me exactly what he had tried as his REI.

Albert said that every time he pretended that he was not afraid to fly, his gut told him he was lying. And when he tried to picture himself making an airline reservation, he felt such intense panic that he had to put the whole thing out of his mind to relieve his anxiety.

When I asked Albert what he meant by "pretending," he explained: "You know, like trying to think positively. I mean, I might think about how beautiful the place that I want to go is, or what I plan to wear, rational stuff like that. And it would work okay until I thought about actually making my reservation. Then like magic, that old feeling that the plane is going to crash would just take over; I could even see me lying there among the dead bodies. And I would feel so anxious that I just couldn't think about it anymore. So I'd stop and try it again later. But it never worked."

ALBERT'S THREE COMMON ERRORS

Like most sane, intelligent people, before Albert was introduced to the Five Rational Questions, he assumed that rational thinking was the kind he did; therefore, irrational thinking had to be the kind other people were doing when they disagreed with him. But when

I introduced Albert to the Five Rational Questions and the result-ing rational thinking, they both sounded logical and good to him; he understood both and immediately agreed with them. Then Albert made this very common error. He assumed that because he understood and agreed with the idea of rational thinking, he must already be doing it. So he understandably used his ideas about it for doing his version of REI.

Albert's second and even more egregious error was assuming that rational thinking is the same as positive thinking. But that's just not so. There is both rational positive thinking and irrational positive thinking. Checking the thinking with the Five Rational Questions (see Chapter 1) is the only way you can tell which is which.

Albert's third error was acting out his attitude that he could trick himself into feeling better about flying *without* really thinking bet-ter about it.* That common mistake is probably the main barrier to success in doing REI.

Why was I so sure that was Albert's attitude? That was his clear-est behavioral message (i.e., message communicated by his be-havior). That is, he acted as if that was his attitude. He said that every time he *pretended* that he was not afraid, his gut (i.e., his emotions) told him that he was lying. He also said that he would still get his old frightening mental scenes of the plane crashing and of him being killed. But the alligator story made the next two important facts quite clear: *Healthy human brains trigger logical reac-tions only to people's real beliefs and attitudes, not the ones they pretend to have.* And healthy human brains are *never* fooled.

Albert continued to have his dreaded mental scenes for one and only one reason: He continued to have the belief and attitude that crashing and dying were most likely to happen to him if he ever flew. Only if Albert had a serious brain disorder could he have felt calm about flying while mentally picturing his dreaded scenes.

But what is the main defect in thinking that people like Albert have? They don't clearly understand the big difference between pretense and practice. That's why I advise such people to memo-

---

*Thinking better about flying would have meant replacing his unlikely belief about crashing and being killed with the much more likely belief that he would safely fly.

rize the following three guidelines that tell you when you are *practicing* a new emotion, instead of just *pretending* to feel it.

1. You are practicing a new emotion when you actually do REI's. That means you sincerely imagine yourself thinking rational thoughts and having only the emotional feelings and physical actions that are rational for those thoughts. In short, you mentally picture yourself having the thoughts, emotions, and actions that people have who already have the habit you want to learn.

But isn't that pretending, you may ask? No, no, no, it is not. Objective mental practice means mentally picturing yourself thinking, emotionally feeling, and physically acting the way you will automatically think, feel, and act after you learn the habit you want to learn. If you don't do that, you will *never* learn that or any new behavior. That's why mental practice means doing REI.

Remember, healthy human brains treat sincere imagination the same way they treat objective reality. That's why REI is the fastest, safest, and most reliable way to practice any new behavior. Both Evelyn's and Albert's cases clearly demonstrate that fact. In both cases, irrational emotive imagery was all they needed to learn their irrational emotional habit. Evelyn had never seen a real alligator, and Albert had never been on an airplane. Yet with their imaginations alone, they had both learned the worst type of irrational fears—phobias.

2. You are mentally and physically practicing a new emotion *only* when you are thinking the thoughts and you physically act in real life in ways that are logical for the new emotion. It does not matter at all that your thoughts and actions "feel wrong." That "wrong" feeling is just cognitive-emotive dissonance; it's the unavoidable third stage in erasing and replacing undesirable habits with desirable ones. To practice a new emotion you have to ignore your "wrong feelings."

3. You are practicing a new emotion when (after a reasonable period of time of thinking and physically reacting the way people think and react who already have that emotional habit) you begin to automatically feel emotionally and react physically in your desired new ways. Those automatic reactions *never* come first; they *always* come last, regardless of the behavior you are practicing. Otherwise, you would *not* need to practice. Remembering those facts will make it easy to learn how to cope better with anything at any time.

When people pretend to improve their emotional control, they either skip guideline #1, or give up with guideline #2. Therefore they never get the rewards of guideline #3. Now let's look at why people get confused in the first place.

Why Do People Confuse Pretense with Practice?

It's mainly because pretending and practicing look alike to the casual eye. To *pretend* to have an emotional habit, you have to act the way people act who already have that emotional habit. And to *practice* a new emotional habit, you also have to act the way people act who already have that emotional habit; otherwise, you will never learn that new habit. Now let's look at the often overlooked but important difference between pretense and practice.

You are pretending when you *retain* and *react* emotionally to the same old attitudes and beliefs that you have always reacted to in the old situations. But you are practicing if you have already con- sciously *replaced your old beliefs* about the old situations *with the rational ideas that people have* who already have learned the new emotional habit you are practicing. When you practice, therefore, you have congruency of sincere thoughts, logical mental scenes, and the other reactions that are most logical for them. Those are essential features of all new emotional and physical learning. Now let's apply those insights to Albert's case.

I asked Albert: "Tell me, can you think of any circumstances in which you would *not* be afraid to fly?"

He thought for a few minutes, then said, "No, I really can't. No matter how you cut it, I still end up feeling that the plane that I get on is going to crash and I actually see my dead body."

Obviously, the only congruence Albert had was between his undesirable mental scenes, his sincere but frightening thoughts, and his undesirable fear and refusal to fly. Understandably, there- fore, his phobia had to persist. In fact, as long as Albert sincerely believed that the plane he got on was going to crash, he would have had to be crazy or brain damaged or suicidal or all three to feel calm about flying.

But Albert was sane, free of brain damage, and he sincerely wanted to live to a ripe old age. So the solution to his phobia was clear—he had to take the following:

Cognitive-Behavioral Prescription for Phobias

The presciption: Use the Five Rational Questions as needed to replace your irrational *possibility* thinking with *rational probability* thinking; then do daily REI, as detailed later in this chapter, plus real-life practice until you are automatically getting your new desired reactions with little or no conscious thought.

Next, you will see how clearly Albert demonstrated the following obvious (but often ignored) fact of human life: Self-control is just as irrational for people who know but ignore obvious, relevant facts as it is for people who are completely ignorant of them. Or, as Albert later reflected: "You know, irrational gut thinking makes idiots of us all, doesn't it?"

ME: "Is the idea that the plane you fly in will crash and kill you based on obvious facts as best you know them?"

ALBERT: "No, the obvious statistical facts say that my plane probably won't crash; but I just have this feeling that it's going to, anyway."

ME: "Well, any sane, intelligent person would have the same feeling if they sincerely imagined the events that you imagine. But how likely are those events, as far as you know?"

ALBERT: "Right. I mean, I know that I'm much more likely to die in an automobile accident on the way to the airport than on a flight; but that fact doesn't help me."

ME: "That fact can't help you until you become willing to think seriously about it at the right time, namely when you are giving yourself a panic attack. But the only time you think about it is when you are talking about it in therapy, like now, or when you are joking about it with a friend."

Author's Note: Albert has just shown you the main reason many self-help book readers *don't* help themselves much, or at all. So please remember it and avoid it.

Most self-help book readers refuse to include in their self-controlling thoughts the new helpful facts they have learned. Instead these readers continue to think in their same old problem-creating ways, yet they are surprised and disappointed when they continue to feel and react in their same old undesirable ways.

Such self-help book readers are like motorists who discover that they are driving down the wrong highway; they take out their road map and carefully read what road changes they need to make to get where they want to go; then they proudly put the road map away and continue to drive down the same, obviously wrong road they had been following; then they angrily complain when they do not arrive at their desired destination. But that's not all. These readers then conclude that because that road map "did not work for them," they should buy a new one at the next gas station, and they do it.

The analogy may sound humorous, even silly; that's because it is. But in my experience, that's exactly the way most people who fail to benefit from reading self-help books think and act. Now let's get back to Albert and the Five Rational Questions.

ME: "Is the idea that your plane will crash likely to help you protect your life and health?"

ALBERT: "No, it doesn't even apply, because I know that commercial flights are much safer than my car; and I ride in my car every day."

ME: "Does believing your idea about a plane crash best help you achieve your goal of overcoming your phobia?"

ALBERT: "Just the opposite. It keeps my phobia going."

ME: "What about helping you avoid conflict with others?"

ALBERT: "It doesn't usually apply to that one."

ME: "Does it best help you feel the emotions you want to feel without alcohol or other drugs?"

ALBERT: "No, it makes me miserably depressed to know that I have such a childish fear. Sometimes I even have to take pills for my depression. But they don't seem to work either."

ME: "So how rational would you say your ideas are about flying?"

ALBERT: "Totally irrational; I've known that all along, but it hasn't helped me. Why is that?"

ME: "Your knowledge hasn't helped you because you have refused to use your knowledge to get yourself to think and react differently about flying. Instead, you ignore your knowledge and insist on acting like a man who is voluntarily holding his hand on a hot stove, but who is both surprised and angry because the stove is burning him. In addition, he knows the easy solution to his problem is to take his hand off the stove. But his knowledge doesn't help him because he refuses to think, I shall take my hand off this stove right now and keep it off, so that it won't hurt anymore."

ALBERT (laughing): "Yes, I see what you mean. But a stove is physical, and the man would know that he is causing his own pain by holding his hand on it. But I don't see what that has to do with me and my fear."

ME: "You insist on holding on to your irrationally fearful beliefs about flying, which trigger both your mental scenes of your plane crashing and your fear that keeps you from flying. In that sense you are acting like the man in the story who has his hand on the hot stove. Do you see that now?"

ALBERT: "Yeah, I think so. You're saying that all I do is picture my plane crashing, which is true; and I do it, even though I know that the plane probably won't crash, which is also true; and that makes what I'm doing irrational, which I've known all along."

ME: "Right! That's stage one in solving your problem. It's called intellectual insight. But as you have proven, insight alone won't solve your problem. You've got to practice your intellectual insight until it becomes emotional insight."

Author's Note: I reviewed again the four other stages in emotional reeducation with Albert. And again, I reviewed the A,B,C's of his panic; and again, I prescribed that he write a REI script. But this time, I insisted that he do it and let me read it before he left my office.

ALBERT'S REI SCRIPT FOR FLYING

My fear of flying is irrational and I refuse to maintain this irrational fear any longer. Flying on commercial airplanes is much safer than riding in my car. So I shall use the Instant Better Feeling Maneuver to keep myself rationally calm while I do REI on calmly making reservations and calmly flying to Hawaii, week after next.

After that session, Albert began doing intensive daily REI's. Intensive REI means REI's for two to ten minutes every morning and evening, plus six to eight more times throughout the day.

Figure 9–5. Two Days Later

Albert also did REI with his eyes open as he drove to and from work, while he was standing in his lunch line, while doing routine tasks at home like washing his car, his clothes, his dishes. With every REI Albert was practicing becoming a person who calmly flies and enjoys it.

Albert had an enjoyable first flight all the way to Hawaii. But that did not mean he could safely stop doing his daily REI's. For long-standing irrational fears such as Albert's, Linda's, and Evelyn's, I recommend daily REI for six to eight weeks after beginning to achieve the desired success. By doing that and refusing to ever go back to thinking or reacting to their highly scored YUPI items, most people can safely stop doing daily REI's on a specific problem after actually experiencing six to eight weeks of personally desired success.

Personally desired success—that's the *only* reliable stop sign for new behavioral practice. That sign varies from person to person. My advice, therefore, is to forget about what most people do; just practice until you achieve your personally desired success. If you decide six to eight weeks are not enough, or if you begin to back-slide, do more practice for as long as it takes you to get and keep the success you want. Isn't that what you do with every other skill? Skill in coping better works exactly the same way.

CORRECT REI ROUTINE

First, copy and memorize the prescribed REI script that accom-panies the one or two YUPI items you plan to erase and replace at that time. Or use the Five Rational Questions (as will be demonstrated in Chapter 12) and write your own REI script, then memorize and use it.

Second, get into a comfortable position, either sitting or lying down with your eyes open or closed. Put a warm, soft smile on your face and use the Instant Better Feeling Maneuver* to make yourself pleasantly calm. Then mentally picture the real-life situation with which you want to cope better. Next, begin silently repeating the rational thoughts in your REI script and, as vividly as possible, imagine yourself feeling emotionally and reacting physically in the most logical way for your REI script. Throughout the experience, keep your warm, soft smile on your face as you breathe at your slow relaxing pace.

Third, do REI for from two to ten minutes—longer if you like—but at least two minutes every time.

Fourth, do REI at the beginning and end of each day and immediately before your lunch and your evening meal, the more often than that the better—your progress will be proportionately faster.

Fifth, limit the number of different REI scripts to one for any two-to-ten-minute REI session. Continue to do REI using the same scripts for at least three consecutive days before you go to a new REI script.

Sixth, do not expect to have erased and replaced any YUPI item in just three days. But move on to your new REI script, if you have one. The erasing and replacing process that you will have started will continue automatically, as long as you are doing daily REI on any personal problem.

Seventh, continue that three-day REI routine until you have done three days of REI using each of the REI scripts you will have written for each of your problems.

Eighth, at every opportunity, act out your REI scripts in your everyday life.

Ninth, after completing three days of REI on each of your REI scripts, repeat those eight steps. But this time focus only on the REI scripts for which you will have *not* yet gained emotional insights. After that, keep on repeating those eight steps until you have gained all of the better coping skills you want.

*That's the slow breathing maneuver (described in Chapter 3) without the Universally Calming Perspective.

The Two Strongest Human Fears

Many intelligent but poorly coping people often irrationally refuse to ever learn to cope better. They naively make themselves victims of the two strongest human fears: fear of being proven wrong and fear of the unknown. Next you'll see why and how they do it.

For these poorly coping people, the ability to cope better is an unknown state, so they frighten themselves with "scary" thoughts such as, Wouldn't it be terrible if I do all that work to learn to cope better but not be any happier? Or, What if I later find out that the way I'm coping now was right all along? Wouldn't that make me look stupid? I couldn't stand it.

Daily REI is the best way to cope with those irrational fears. Why? Because realistically imagining, i.e., vicarious learning, is one of the healthiest ways to cope with life. For example, most sane, intelligent people don't have to go to jail before deciding that it's best to stay out of there. Realistic imagination is all they need for that decision. Similarly, realistically imagining what coping better is like is the best way to convince yourself that it's good to end up doing it. Realistically imaging yourself actually doing rational things is Rational Emotive Imagery—REI.

Once when I made that point in a public speech, a poorly coping graduate student in philosophy posed this question: "But if I am only one of those FHB's or fallible human beings, Dr. Maultsby, that you like to emphasize, how can I be sure that it's *not* wrong for me to change how I'm now reacting? After all, as you pointed out, Dr. Maultsby, people don't learn habits that they believe are wrong at the time they learn them. So at one time I must have believed that my present reactions were not wrong. Wouldn't you say that's right, Dr. Maultsby?"

My answer was: "Yes, you are right. That's why it is so important for you to make these two helpful insights: Just like everybody else, *all of your reactions now are still right for your present life experiences. And again, just like everybody else, you don't have to be wrong to change your present reactions. The only two things you need are: the desire for a different life experience and the sanity to know that you cannot get a different life experience if you insist on thinking, acting, and reacting as you are doing now."*

So it's not a question of whether or not behaving as you do is wrong for you. The only question is: Do you want a change in your present life experiences? If you answer: "Yes, I do," then learning to cope better will certainly be right for you. So go for it with REI.

Memory Aid Questions for Chapter 9

1. What is the correct REI routine?
2. What are the two main reasons REI may not help people?
3. How long is it *best* to do daily REI's?
4. What is the necessary relationship between positive thinking and rational thinking?
5. Positive thinking is always rational. True or False?
6. Rational thinking does not have to be positive. True or False?
7. When are you practicing a new emotional habit, what do you have to do that may make it appear that you are just pretending?
8. When people are only pretending to improve their emotional control what do they do?
9. Why is it so easy to confuse pretending to improve one's emotional control with practicing the new emotional control one desires?
10. What is one of the main reasons readers of self-help books don't help themselves?
11. What unrealistic expectation do many self-help book readers have?
12. Albert already knew all he needed to know to get rid of his flying phobia. He was just ignoring his knowledge, or refusing to think about it at the right time. True or False?
13. Describe how and why the analogy of the hot stove fit Albert's behavior.
14. REI is just healthy *(a)* _____; but REI enables you to learn new *(b)* _____ habits in the *(c)* _____, *(d)* _____, and most reliable *(e)* _____ because healthy undrugged *(f)* _____ treat *(g)* _____ imagination as if it were *(h)* _____ reality.

Answers appear in Appendix II.

SECTION IV

Guaranteeing Your Success in Coping Better

CHAPTER 10: **Normal Irrational Illusions (NII's)**—This chapter will explain why human brains instantly convert sincere illusions into life experience and discusses two irrational illusions.

CHAPTER 11: **Three More Normal Irrational Illusions**—This chapter desribes three more normal irrational illusions.

CHAPTER 12: **Guaranteeing Your Success in Coping Better**—This chapter will reveal how to make sure that you are not unwittingly working against yourself and how you can erase two main causes of poor coping.

CHAPTER 13: **The Value of Rational Rhetoric**—Five more common sense beliefs are discussed, with a special focus on the logic and value of using rational rhetoric.

There are five extremely harmful pyschoemotional pollutants that parents all over the world usually teach their children. Unfortunately, those parents almost never teach their children the Five Rational Questions for healthy thinking. Predictably, therefore, virtually all children enter adulthood believing to some degree that these psychoemotional pollutants are objective facts.

That phenomenon is so universal, I call those five psycho-emotional pollutants Normal Irrational Illusions or NII's. At least one of these irrational ideas is a core mechanism in most people's failures to cope better in their lives.

CHAPTER 10

Normal Irrational Illusions (NII's)

Instantly Helpful Insights

An illusion is an inaccurate perception of some objectively real event.

Evelyn's illusion was her perception of that harmless rubber alligator being a dangerous creature. But healthy brains don't care whether or not people's illusions fit the obvious facts. Healthy brains just instantly convert people's sincere illusions into the corresponding life experiences those people would have had if their illusions had been facts.

Special Vocabulary for Chapter 10

Anger.   The normal human urge to harm or destroy, at least momentarily, the objects of that urge.

Choice.   Any instance of voluntary action, even if the action is taken in response to a threat.

Forced.   Being physically overpowered and therefore having no alternative voluntary action.

Jehovah complex.   The habit of getting undesirably angry or feeling undesirable guilt (i.e., punitive self-anger) because personal life events are not the way the concerned person believes they should or ought to be.

Irrational anger.   Any more of the urge to harm or destroy than helps one cope with a given situation better than remaining calm would help him or her cope with it.

Magic.   Any imaginary force that is supposed to make events occur in the real world (outside human minds) *without* anyone or anything first doing what is objectively necessary to make those events occur.

Magical thinking.   The belief or the attitude that merely the act of wanting some event strongly enough can make that event occur.

Personalize.   To express ideas about oneself with the first person "I" instead of with the second person "you" or the third person "one" or "people."

Rational anger.   The least amount of the urge to harm or destroy that best helps one cope with a given situation. (Most often rational anger is no more irritation than sane, intelligent people need to motivate themselves to kill a bothersome fly or mosquito.)

TGIF syndrome.   The habit of relieving job-related anger by sincerely thinking, Thank goodness it's Friday and I don't have to work anymore this week. This syndrome is quite different from the popular but meaningless TGIF cliche that even happy workers jokingly parrot.

TGIW good feeling. The good feeling triggered by the sincere thought, Thank goodness I'm working. It's the most effective cure for the TGIF (Thank goodness it's Friday) syndrome.

True believer. A person who would score an idea higher than 2 on the YUPI scale.

Important Questions Answered in Chapter 10

1. Why should all of the present things or events that now exist in the real world (outside human minds) be exactly as they are?*
2. What do common, everyday *should* ideas really mean?
3. What are the rational versus the irrational concepts of *should*?
4. How does irrational anger reinforce irrational *should* ideas?
5. What's the best way to prevent or get rid of the TGIF syndrome and the job-burnout problems it causes?
6. What's the real reason sane, intelligent people work?
7. Is anyone ever really forced to work?

At first, people often strongly resist accepting the facts in this chapter. To avoid that potential distraction, it's a good idea to have a pencil and paper handy as you read. Then you can jot down your objections immediately and continue reading without fear of forgetting them or without the disadvantage of distracting yourself from their supporting evidence.

NII #1 and It's Rational Analyses

NII #1: Some things or events are so undesirable that they should not ever exist or happen and I get very upset when they do exist or happen. But some other things or events are so desirable that they should always exist or happen and I get very upset when they don't.

---

*If you can think of any exceptions (i.e., things that should not now exist) list those things or events now, and review them after you read this chapter.

OBJECTIVE FACTS ABOUT NII #1

Normal Irrational Illusion #1 is probably the most universally believed bit of magical thinking there is. It is also the irrational illusion that most people most strongly resist erasing and replacing with healthier, more rational ideas. Understandably, therefore, NII #1 probably causes more unhealthy emotional distress than any other psychoemotional pollutant.

To get the most helpful insights into NII #1 and the irrational anger and guilt it causes, first take an objective look at the following insights.

When people angrily think or say that something "should" or "shouldn't" be, what word would they most probably have used if they had not known the words *should* or *ought*? Most probably they would have used the word *want*: "I wanted" or "I didn't want" it to be this way.

Now add that fact to the next two. People almost never get irrationally angry about events that they believe should be exactly the way they are now.* People almost always get irrationally angry about events that they believe should not be the way they are now. But the empirical law of the universe seems to be: *Everything is always exactly as it now should be, even though it's not what I or anyone else wanted to see.*

That seeming law is the operational basis of all empirical science, medicine, physics, chemistry, etc. There could be no empirical science if anything ever could be a way it should not now be. Since this handbook is based on the empirical science of healthy human behavior, I prescribe only the above scientific concept of should.

IRRATIONALLY ANGRY PEOPLE AND THE JEHOVAH COMPLEX

When people are irrationally angry, they are upset because something isn't the way they want it to be, even though they did not do what was necessary to make it that way. Such people are like people who want to make a chocolate cake, but forget to put in the

---

*Keep in mind that irrational anger is more anger than people need to cope better with their situation.

chocolate; yet, they angrily claim that their cake should have been chocolate anyway.

"But," many people ask me, "what if you do what's necessary to get what you want and still don't get it? What then?" Such an event can't happen in the nonmagical world outside people's minds. Failure to make that important insight causes sane, intelligent people to develop a Jehovah complex.

Sane, intelligent, but irrationally angry people do not consciously think, I'm God. But that seems to be their unerased early childhood attitude. I say that because this superconscious, and therefore, unspoken idea, "I'm God," is the most logical explanation for people's irrational anger. Next is the evidence for that statement.

Regardless of people's race or culture, most share this belief: There is a God who has unlimited power and the prerogative of "will" over the universe. Therefore, all a God has to do to make things happen is "will" or want them to happen. In addition, not "willing" or wanting something is sufficient for a God to have intense anger, if the unwanted thing happens anyway. "For great is the wrath of the Lord . . . because our fathers have not harkened unto his words" (*II Kings* 22:13).

Up to the age of three or four years, almost all well-cared-for children get the illusion that they are gods. For the most part, the world certainly seems to exist mainly to anticipate their wills or wants and/or satiate them automatically or in immediate response to their angry cries. Consequently, by the time children are six or seven years old, they usually have learned the lifelong habit of reacting with "God-like" anger when they do not get what they intensely want.

Granted, six- and seven-year-olds usually have already made the healthy adult insight that the world does not exist solely for their pleasure. But without specific systematic mental practice such as is prescribed in this book, people almost never erase and replace completely the childish attitude: "I'm God." Instead, they just hide their Jehovah complex behind socially approved *shoulds* and *shouldn'ts*.

Now keep in mind that in everyday life, angry "shoulds" and "shouldn'ts" are just socially approved equivalents of "I want" or "I don't want." That insight makes the next fact clear.

NII #1 really says: I have decided that some things or events are so undesirable that *I* don't ever want them to exist or happen and I become very upset when they do exist or happen. And some things or events are so desirable that *I* always want them to exist or happen and I become very upset when they don't exist or happen.

But what are the three basic laws of the nonmagical universe that support the scientific concept of *should* described earlier? Here they are:

First, events occur only if what is necessary for them to occur has already been done.

Second, when what's necessary for events to occur has been done, those events must, have to, and therefore, *should* occur and vice versa.

Third, when an event does *not* occur, the most objectively valid explanation is: "What was necessary to make that event occur has not been done yet; therefore, that event cannot and should not occur yet."

To rationally accept these universal laws of life, you must first replace the *magical everyday concept of should* with the *scientific concept of should*, which says: "Everything is always exactly as it now should be, even though it's not what I, or anyone else, wanted to see."

To most quickly get over resistance to accepting the scientific concept of *should*, keep this fact in mind: Without the scientific concept of *should*, there could not be a science of anything; in addition, emotionally healthy living would be impossible.

When most people think objectively about that fact, they instantly see it. Still, at this point, many people develop a hearing defect. They say: "Dr. Maultsby, I hear you saying that people should never get angry or feel guilty or be depressed about anything; but I don't agree with that." My response is: "But I'm not saying that at all; nor would I ever say that. I'm a physician. I only prescribe healthy behaviors. I know that to get angry or otherwise upset sometimes is just as normal and healthy as it is to eat. But as you and I also know, people can and do eat too much, as well as get upset too much. In fact, thousands of people eat *and* upset themselves to death every year."

Even though you consistently use *should* scientifically, you will still get rationally and, therefore, appropriately angry and guilty.

You still will act in your own best interest, too. But scientific *shoulds* won't make you self-defeatingly or otherwise irrationally angry or guilty. Consequently, your negative emotions won't make you sick. In addition, you will work even more effectively than ever before to change what you don't like and to keep what you do like about the things in your life.

THE HAZARD OF MAGICAL *SHOULDS* AND *SHOULDN'TS*

Linda (the "mouse lady") was chronically angry at herself because she believed that she *shouldn't* be a "disgusting, gutless mouse."* In addition, she believed that she *should* behave like a rationally self-controlled adult, even though she had not yet learned that behavior. Therefore, her beliefs would have made rational sense only in a world of magical forces. That's why merely changing from irrational to rational *shoulds* enabled her to quickly start coping better with herself and everything else.

If you doubt the tremendous power of merely changing your mind about your *shoulds*, do this. Imagine that you are angry because you believed someone had not done an important thing for you that he or she had promised to do. Now imagine that while you are still angry, you discover that you have made a mistake— the person really has done what he or she promised to do. What do you know would happen to your anger the instant you discover your mistake?

Your anger would instantly vanish. Or more precisely, you would instantly stop creating your anger. Why? Mainly because you are not silly, idotic, or crazy. Like all sane, intelligent people, you believe it would be silly to continue to feel angry about something that you know is exactly the way it now should be. So merely by changing your mind from the strongly believed but magical idea, "It shouldn't be this way," to the equally strongly believed scientific idea, "What was promised was done; so everything is as

---

*For an excellent discussion of how magical *shoulds* kill self-motivation for self-improvement in all life's areas, read pages 183–188 in my book *Rational Behavior Therapy* (Prentice-Hall, Inc., 1984).

it should now be," you would have instantly replaced your irrational anger with rational happiness.

AN IMPORTANT INSIGHT TO REMEMBER

No, you will not (as instantly as in the example above) switch from poor coping to better coping the first or even fourth or fifth time you mentally replace a NII or YUPI item with the prescribed REI script. Why? Because in the example above, you would have been changing your mind from one strongly believed and well-practiced idea to another equally strongly believed and well-practiced idea. So you would have had the same immediate response potential for both ideas.

In obvious contrast to that situation, you probably will not have practiced the prescribed REI scripts at all. Yet your highly scored NII and YUPI items are already strongly believed and well-practiced ideas. So your present response potentials for them are very much greater than they initially will be for the prescribed REI scripts. You can, however, quickly reverse that situation. But to do that, you will have to go through the five stages of emotional reeducation described in Chapter 8. That takes a little time and diligent REI mental practice.

AN AID FOR PERSONALIZING RAPIDLY

To learn to cope better, you must first personalize your new, more rational ideas. That means using the first person "I" instead of the second person "you" or the third person "one." To help you speed up your personalizing process, I have described the suggested goals and REI scripts for the NII's and YUPI items using the first person "I" instead of the second person "you." As you read these ideas, imagine that they are already yours.* That simple mental

*The REI scripts prescribed in this book have proven to be effective for most people. So you can confidently use them. You are also free to write your own REI scripts. Until you do, however, use the prescribed ones. Also, remember that as soon as you sincerely accept and use the prescribed scripts, they then are just as much yours as any ones you may write.

maneuver will instantly start your emotional reeducational process.

My better coping goal for NII #1 is to mentally erase it and replace it with the facts and rational ideas in my REI script for NII #1. Then I shall use that script for daily REI's as suggested in Chapter 9.

MY PRESCRIBED REI SCRIPT FOR NII #1

I shall now mentally picture myself in a situation where I normally think NII #1, but I shall sincerely think: Everything is always exactly as it now should be, even though it's different from what I wanted to see. So until I can make it the way I want it to be, I shall keep myself pleasantly calm, naturally.* With a warm, soft smile on my face, I shall continue to breathe at my slow, stress-reducing pace, until I am as pleasantly calm naturally as I now think it's best for me to be.

*Actually picture yourself sincerely thinking those rational ideas in your situations of anger. That slow breathing pace is the Instant Better Feeling Maneuver. See Chapter 3.

A FEW PARTING WORDS ABOUT *SHOULDS*

Obviously, keeping your mind clear about the big difference between magical, or irrational, and scientific, or rational *shoulds* is essential for coping better. Next are the nine major differences between those two *should* concepts. Carefully study them over and over until they "feel" right to you.

THE IRRATIONAL VERSUS RATIONAL *SHOULDS* CHECKLIST

1. Irrational *shoulds* refer to what isn't.

1. Rational *shoulds* refer to what is.

2. Irrational *shoulds* are judgmental and subjective.

2. Rational *shoulds* are nonjudgmental and objective.

3. Irrational *shoulds* refer only to what the speakers want, even though the speakers have not done what's necessary to get it.

3. Rational *shoulds* refer only to what had to be, or will have to be, given the preceding circumstances.

4. Irrational *shoulds* inappropriately assume that what the speakers want is always right, and what they don't want is always wrong.

4. Rational *shoulds* recognize that what is right or wrong differs with people, times, and places.

5. Irrational *shoulds* are magical thinking; they imply that things can and ought to exist merely because the speaker wants them to exist, even though what's necessary to make them exist has not yet been done.

5. Rational *shoulds* are conditional and scientific. They recognize that things cannot exist until what's necessary to make them exist has first been done.

6. Irrational *shoulds* trigger unproductive anger toward others and/or inappropriate

6. Rational *shoulds* trigger rational emotions toward others as well as toward oneself.

guilt feelings toward oneself. Therefore, the speakers waste valuable emotional energy that could be used to improve their situation.

That's why calm study of the existing facts and rational decisions about what's best to do usually result.

7. Irrational *shoulds* lead to self-defeating, poor motivation to work at changing what the speakers don't like.

7. Rational *shoulds* lead to ideal self-motivation to work at changing what the speakers don't like.

8. With irrational *shoulds*, the speakers try to get other people to do things without first doing what is necessary to influence them to do it.

8. With rational *shoulds*, the speakers recognize that to get people to do something, the speakers must first do what is necessary to influence them to do it.

9. Irrational *shoulds* say: "It" (namely, what obviously is or obviously exists) "shouldn't be." Then, if "It" is important to the speaker, he or she has a temper tantrum about "It." But the tantrum often takes so much energy that, in emotional self-defense, the speaker forgets the whole event and merely hopes that "It" does not happen again.

9. Rational *shoulds* say: "It" (namely, what obviously is or obviously exists) "is exactly as it now should be, even though it's not what the speakers want to see." And that's why they keep themselves pleasantly calm rationally, until they do what is necessary to make "It" the way they want it to be.

NORMAL EXPERIENCES

When people first switch from their handy-dandy but irrational magical *shoulds* to rational, healthy *shoulds*, they temporarily have a little trouble expressing themselves. But that lasts only until they get used to replacing their irrational *shoulds* with rational ones: "I, (he, she, or they) did exactly what I (he, she, or they) should have, based on my (or their) beliefs at that moment." It's also appropriate to replace irrational *shoulds* with honest "I want, I wish, I think it would be in my best interest, or in your best interest." Just be honest and always say what you really mean, and mean what you say, instead of using irrational *shoulds*. Your communications will immediately become clearer, less emotionally confusing, and, therefore, more effective.

NII #2 and Its Rational Analyses

NII #2: There are certain undesirable things that I hate even the thought of doing; but I do them if and when I have to do them, that is, when I have no choice or I'm forced to do them.

THE OBJECTIVE FACTS ABOUT NII #2

True believers in this NII usually have problems with self-defeating procrastination, the TGIF—thank goodness it's Friday—syndrome, and burnout. The main cause of these three problems is the habit of incorrectly calling one's personal choices to do personally undesirable things "no choice" or "being forced" to do those undesirable things.

The obvious fact is that people *always* choose to do their personally undesirable acts. But unhappy people victimize themselves with this irrational habit: They sincerely call two or more undesirable choices "no choice." And to healthy brains, the idea of having "no choice" is the same as "I'm forced" or "I have to." Also, healthy human brains don't care whether or not people are forced or have to, as they claim. If people believe that they have "no choice" or "I have to" or "I'm forced," those beliefs cause healthy brains to create the same angry, resistive feelings they would have if they really were forced to act. Therefore, the first step in the rational solution to procrastination, TGIF syndrome, and burnout is for the victims to focus on the following five facts:

1. Objectively, choice means having two or more voluntary ways to react to a given situation. It's irrelevant that those ways of reacting are personally undesirable, or that someone is coercing you with threats. Whether to react and how you react will still be your choice.*

2. Having two or more *desirable* choices is relatively rare in everyday life. In fact, when most people get two or more equally

*Fortunately, in civilized countries people are protected by law from illegal coercion, so criminal acts are not covered here.

desirable choices, they usually are so surprised that they become pleasantly confused. Often they will ask some other person: "Which one should I choose?" Or, out of fear of not getting another such desirable choice, they try to choose all of the desirable alternatives at the same time.

3. Objectively, being forced to act means being physically restrained from any voluntary action in a given situation.

4. The normal and natural human reactions to being forced are intense self-dislike and at least symbolic, if not physical, resistance to compliance. The most common forms of symbolic resistance are compliance with overt or covert anger and/or defective performance, most commonly called "goldbricking."

5. The normal natural human reactions to *admittedly* choosing even between two or more of their most hated alternatives is at worst only mild irritation. Even then, the person still has the self-satisfaction of knowing that he or she was smart enough to make the lesser of two or more personally undesirable choices.

Why is that knowledge self-satisfying? Intelligent people know that much of emotionally healthy and personally satisfying living is nothing more than calmly choosing between the lesser of two or more undesirables. That's why such a choice can sometimes be an even healthier reason for feeling good about oneself than the choice between two or more desirables.*

*Often the choice between two or more desirable events is frankly harmful. A good example is a cigarette-addicted patient with emphysema having and making the choice between two or more personally desirable brands of cigarettes.

Now compare the hated self-image of being forced to the healthy self-image people have who see themselves as choosing to act.

Intelligent people do personally *un*desirable things for only two reasons: to get the personal benefits they hope their action will produce, and to get the healthy self-image of acting in their own best interest.

People who believe they are being forced see themselves as being impotent, mindless objects of the benevolent or malevolent whimsical manipulations of other, more powerful people or events. That is probably the most hated self-image sane, intelligent people ever have. Yet they *always* get it to some degree every time they sincerely think: "I am forced to . . . " or "I had no choice . . . " or "I have to . . . "

FOUR HEALTHY REASONS FOR ALWAYS OWNING UP TO YOUR CHOICES

First, when you admittedly choose to do the lesser of two undesirables, you can not dislike yourself or angrily resist doing it. Why?

First, because sane, intelligent people do undesirable tasks *only when they believe they are acting in their own best interest; and sane, intelligent people do not resist or dislike themselves for admittedly acting in their own best interest.*

Second, if you frequently remind yourself of the personal benefits you hope your chosen action will produce, you will prevent or quickly solve the problems of self-defeating procrastination and resentment associated with doing undesirable tasks.

Third, by frequently reminding yourself of the personal benefits you hope your chosen action will produce, you will prevent or quickly solve TGIF syndrome and the job burnout it causes.* Why? Because both TGIF syndrome and job burnout are the direct results of chronic anger and depression triggered by people's beliefs that they are forced to work instead of having chosen to work at their jobs.

Those facts point to a highly effective yet very simple solution to TGIF syndrome and job burnout. Just start every workday with the sincere TGIW (thank goodness I'm working) insight. Then repeat it every time someone else says TGIF.

THE REALITY ABOUT WORKING PEOPLE

Throughout human history people have always worked only because they chose to work. That fact of normal human behavior was described over two thousand years ago with: ". . . they that labor, labor for themselves because their mouths crave it of them" (*Proverbs* 16:26).

In other words, people choose to work because of the personal benefits they hope their work will produce. Hoped-for personal benefits can be a more powerful self-motivating force than even hunger. The many people who voluntarily fast to protest current undesirable situations continually prove that fact. This explains why just frequently reminding yourself of your hoped-for benefits is the quickest and the most permanent cure for procrastination, TGIF syndrome, all "burnouts," and poor motivation in general.

---

*Remember, TGIF syndrome is quite different from the widely popular but meaningless TGIF cliché that even happy workers jokingly parrot.

Thinking: "TG I W" works faster and better if you think it with a warm soft smile on your face.

Fourth, every moment you keep yourself free of undesirable anger and resentment is another moment you have available for natural happiness and/or coping better with your life.

My better coping goal for NII #2 is to mentally erase it and replace it with the facts in my REI script for NII #2. Therefore, I shall use that script for my daily REI's, as suggested in Chapter 9.

MY PRESCRIBED REI SCRIPT FOR NII #2

I shall now mentally picture myself in a situation where I normally think NII #2, but I shall sincerely think: Everything I do, I do solely because I choose to do it. I choose to perform this particular undesirable act because I hope to get these personal benefits. (Then actually list and mentally picture yourself getting the personal benefits you hope to get from doing that particular act.)

Congratulations

You are now ready to begin using the correct REI routine described in Chapter 9. Regardless of how you might have scored the NII's, do REI on each of them for three consecutive days. And remember, be patient with yourself. Trouble really is the only thing people reliably get fast and easy, the very first time.

THREE FACTS TO REMEMBER

1. Everything is always exactly as it now should be, even though it's different from what I, or anyone else, wanted to see.
2. Everything you do, you do *only* because you choose to do it; otherwise, you refuse to do it.
3. Your healthy brain doesn't care: It will instantly give you any irrational and self-defeating or healthy and better coping life experience that's right for the sincere words you choose to use to think.

Three Instantly Helpful Insights to Act on Daily

1. To feel better emotionally, without alcohol or other drugs, you must perceive, believe, and react better.

2. Where your healthy as well as naturally happy emotional control and better coping skills are concerned, it's never just semantics, *it's always all semantics*. So, think only what is really best for you to think. That's always a rational idea.

3. If you are neither joking nor lying, your normal, healthy brain will instantly convert your thoughts into the most logical, conscious life experiences for your thoughts. And your life experiences of the moment are the only realities you can know and react to; so, why not make them as rational, and therefore helpful, as you can.

Author's Note: On their first exposure to NII's #1 and 2, people almost never have the ideally helpful emotional reactions. They either react with too much or too little emotion. But these NII's influence us all. I suggest, therefore, that you do *not* read any further today. Instead, use your remaining reading time to review these insights and rethink them rationally (i.e., using the Five Rational Questions—see Chapter 1), and give particular rational attention to any objections you may now have to any aspect of them.

Memory Aid Questions for Chapter 10

1. An (a) _____ is an inaccurate perception of an objectively (b) _____ event.
2. Evelyn's panic response was in reaction to the (a) _____ that a (b) _____ alligator was (c) _____.
3. It's accurate to say that you were (a) _____ only when you were (b) _____ overpowered.
4. It is accurate to use the word _____ even when the choices are all undesirable.
5. The (a) _____ complex means the person gets undesirably angry in response to his or her (b) _____ and *shouldn'ts*.
6. TGIW means: "Thank (a) _____ I'm (b) _____." When TGIW is (c) _____, it cures the (d) _____ syndrome.
7. People almost (a) _____ get angry when they believe that (b) _____ is as it (c) _____ be.
8. The main causes of the Jehovah complex and irrational guilt are irrational (a) _____ and (b) _____ .

9. NII #1 really means things *(a)* _____ be exactly
   the way I *(b)* _____ or *(c)* _____
   them to be.

10. In reality everything is *(a)* _____ exactly the
    way it *(b)* _____ be now.

11. But nothing has to *(a)* _____ the way it now
    (b) _____ .

12. Past the age of three or four years, it's very
    (a) _____ that anyone is ever
    (b) _____ to do anything.

13. People who have TGIF syndrome need to
    (a) _____ themselves often of the personal
    (b) _____ their jobs give
    (c) _____.

14. Everyone, including slaves, works only because
    they _____ to work.

15. "They that labor *(a)* _____ for
    (b) _____ because their *(c)* _____
    crave it of *(d)* _____ " is one of the
    (e) _____ recorded insights into
    (f) _____ human behavior.

16. To feel better emotionally without alcohol or other
    (a) _____ , you must *(b)* _____
    better.

17. It's *(a)* _____ just semantics where your
    (b) _____ control is concerned, it's all
    (c) _____.

18. If you are neither *(a)* _____ nor
    (b) _____, your healthy *(c)* _____
    instantly converts your statements into your current life
    (d) _____.

Answers appear in Appendix II.

CHAPTER 11

Three More Normal Irrational Illusions

Instantly Helpful Insights

Often the most obviously incorrect illusions are the ones people most strongly resist giving up. Linda (the "mouse lady" in Chapter 7) clearly demonstrated that fact.

Don't be surprised if you seem to have less resistance to giving up the next three NII's than you had to giving up NII's #1 and 2. For most people that appearance of less resistance is just an illusion. So please pay as much attention to erasing and replacing these NII's as you do to NII's #1 and 2.

Special Vocabulary for Chapter 11

False. Any idea that can be objectively shown to misrepresent the facts of a situation.

Fantasy. A scene in a person's mind's eye that is triggered by thoughts that do not accurately fit the obvious facts of a situation.

Obvious facts. Objectively real events and descriptions of such events that accurately duplicate the way video cameras or other mechanical recording devices would record or show the real events. The antonym for obvious facts is *nonfactual*; the synonym is *correct*.

Important Questions Answered in Chapter 11

1. How will you know when you are describing obvious fact instead of a normal irrational illusion?
2. "As people think in their hearts, so are they," *Proverbs* 23:7. What does that three-thousand-year-old insight into normal human behavior mean?
3. Are some people more fallible than others?
4. What is the only reality you can ever completely control or even know?
5. Can you describe anything that is objectively awful or terrible?
6. With reference to your behavior, why is it best to think of yourself the way you would think of an orange tree?

NII #3 and Its Rational Analysis

NII #3: People (including me) are the same as their behavior.

THE OBJECTIVE FACTS ABOUT NII #3

True believers in this illusion usually have a poor self-image. They often refer to themselves with negative labels such as "idiot," "stupid," "worthless," "fat slob," "gutless mouse," and so forth. Such self-labels can't ever pass the Camera Check of Perceptions. Linda is a good example of that fact.

Linda responded to the negative name of her illusion, "gutless mouse," as if she were that thing. Such painfully negative names are forms of self-punishment. People who use them believe or have the attitude that self-punishment will make them change their behavior enough for them (in their minds) to stop deserving those negative names. Unfortunately, although self-punishment almost never produces permanent behavior change, it usually does produce useless emotional pain.

The first step in solving that problem is to realize that people are somewhat like orange trees.

Sane, intelligent orange tree owners would not label a healthy orange tree rotten and cut it down (nor in any other way abuse it) just because the tree had a few rotten oranges on it. Instead, sane, intelligent orange tree owners would improve their care of the oranges and happily keep the healthy orange tree just as it is. The owners would realize that an orange tree is not the same as its oranges.

Similarly, the Camera Check of Perceptions helps people clearly see the next point: Their fallible human state never changes, regardless of how well or poorly they behave. That's why frequent Camera Checks stop people from downing, damning, or denigrating themselves with inaccurate labels. These people then see that they are not the same as their behaviors. That's why even a host of "rotten" behaviors cannot change a person into a "rotten person." There is only one type of human being—FHB's, fallible human beings. Consequently, rationally thinking people always give themselves unconditional, positive self-acceptance. Why? Because they see that they are all they have and all they need to give themselves a naturally happy life. That insight leads to calmly, instead of miserably, concentrating on improving one's "rotten" behaviors. The man in the following illustration, for example, learned that fact by concentrating on this important insight: We humans differ only in how often we clearly demonstrate our fallibility with "rotten" behaviors.

My better coping goal for NII #3 is to mentally erase it and replace it with the facts in my REI script for NII #3. Therefore, I shall use that script for my daily REI's, as suggested in Chapter 9.

MY PRESCRIBED REI SCRIPT FOR NII #3

I shall now mentally picture myself in a situation where I normally think NII #3, but I shall sincerely think: All human beings are just FHB's—fallible human beings. So, that's what I have always been; that's what I am now; and that's what I shall always be. Therefore, no matter how desirably, or undesirably, I behave, I shall always be only an FHB, just like everybody else. That's why FHB and my legal name are the only self-labels that correctly apply to me and the only ones I shall use. That's also why I shall always give myself unconditional, positive self-acceptance as a person, regardless of what I do.

NII #4 and Its Rational Analysis

NII #4: It makes me angry that I can't do certain things that other people with my abilities easily do, such as say no to people or kill harmless bugs.

THE OBJECTIVE FACTS ABOUT NII #4

True believers in NII #4 usually mislabel their irrational fears as personal inabilities. Linda, "the mouse lady," gave you a good example of NII #4. She said that she couldn't say no to people; yet she obviously did say no to people, anytime she was not too afraid to say it.

NII #4 usually causes self-dislike. Here's how these people justify their self-dislike: They believe: "I must be inferior to the people who can easily do those simple things that I can't do. If I were not inferior, I could do them too. But I can't; and I just can't accept myself being inferior."

Again like Linda, however, these people's *real* problem is being irrationally afraid of doing the things they angrily claim they "can't do," even though they often do them when they think it's "safe."

My better coping goal for NII #4 is to mentally erase it and replace it with the facts in my REI script for NII #4. Therefore, I shall use that script for my daily REI's, as suggested in Chapter 9.

MY PRESCRIBED REI SCRIPT FOR NII #4

I shall now mentally picture myself in a situation where I normally think NII #4, but I shall sincerely think: I can do the things I used to irrationally think I couldn't do. It's just that my irrational fears kept me from doing them. But now I insist on acting out my new, rational ideas about those things. That's why every day I do this REI to practice calmly doing what I can and want to do in real life. And, whenever it's practical, I actually act that way in real life.

NII #5 and Its Rational Analysis

NII #5: Some people as well as some life events are just plain terrible or awful; there are just no other words for them; and I can't stand either those people or those events.

THE OBJECTIVE FACTS ABOUT NII #5

There aren't any objectively terrible or awful events in real life. Instead, so-called awful and terrible events are like beauty; they exist—never in the real world—but only in the mind's eye of the person who imagines them.

Here's how you can quickly prove that fact yourself. Try to think of a single life event in the history of human life that you believe is or was terrible or awful. Does every other equally sane, intelligent person agree with you? If you answer "Yes," that will mean that you believe that there is no equally sane, intelligent person like you anywhere, who believes that your "terrible or awful" event is or was both "right and appropriate, if not great." I doubt that you believe that. But even if you do believe it, I think you probably will agree that most people's "awful's" and "terribles" are only some other people's "inconvenience's," or even "good's." That's why it's usually best to remember:

> Healthy brains don't care what people imagine, believe, and then perceive as if it were objectively real. But healthy brains will always give people a seemingly "awful" or "terrible" emotional feeling for any idea or situation that they sincerely think is awful or terrible.

Unfortunately, naive, gut-thinking people believe their real "awful" or "terrible" emotional feelings prove that the event they perceive is an objectively awful or terrible event. But that's not all. Depending on how miserable these people feel, they often do as Linda did: decide that they just can't stand that awful or terrible event anymore and try to kill themselves, or someone else. Even then, however, all they prove is that irrational illusions can lead sane, intelligent people to try to kill themselves or others.

The things people really *can't* stand actually do kill them. So the next time you say that you can't stand something that either you or other people with your abilities have survived, point out to yourself that past survival usually indicates ability to survive and, therefore, stand the event now.

Granted, you may have stood similar past events miserably; and you may even be miserably standing the event now. But miserably standing something is still standing it. And if you would just rationally control yourself, you would probably stand it less miserably now.

My better coping goal for NII #5 is to mentally erase it and replace it with the facts in my REI script for NII #5. Therefore, I shall use that script for my daily REI's.

MY PRESCRIBED REI SCRIPT FOR NII #5

I shall now mentally picture myself in a situation where I normally think NII #5, but I shall sincerely think: Objectively speaking, one person's "awful" and/or "terrible" can be someone else's "good" or even "great." My present situation is not objectively awful or terrible; it's merely undesirable and/or inconvenient; maybe it's even very, very undesirable and/or inconvenient for me. But if I do not want to tolerate it, I can and shall do what I think is best to change it; and fortunately, I don't have to waste my emotional energy feeling "awful" or "terrible" about it before I change it.

When I say that something is awful or terrible, I don't get any more useful information than I get when I say that thing is very, very, very undesirable and/or inconvenient for me. Also, If I believe anything is awful or terrible, I force myself to feel much worse than I would feel if I honestly admitted that even the worst events in my life are only very, very, very, very, very, very, very undesirable and/or inconvenient for me. Since I prefer to feel better, I shall think better by eliminating the misleading words *awful* and *terrible* from my vocabulary of serious thoughts. For joking and lying, however, those words will still be hard to beat.

AN IMPORTANT FACT TO REMEMBER

You are *not* your "rotten" behavior. Therefore, it's irrational to make yourself feel rotten about it.

Memory Aid Questions for Chapter 11

1. Many of the ideas that everybody in a given culture learns to
   (a) _____ can not pass the
   (b) _____ Check of *(c)* _____
   reality.
2. What are the three NII's discussed in this chapter?
3. What's best to do if, in spite of your three days of REI, you
   still have evidence of the influence of your old NII''s?
4. Why were the REI scripts and better coping goals written
   using the first person "I" instead of the second person
   "You"?
5. People really are the same as their behavior. True or False?
6. Describe the orange tree analogy and the important insights
   it gives you.
7. Can anyone be more or less fallible than anyone else? Yes or
   No?
8. State the reason for your answer to question #7.
9. Is there anything that's objectively awful or terrible?
10. It doesn't make *(a)* _____ to feel awful or
    terrible about something that objectively is only
    (b) _____ or maybe only very, very, very, very,
    very *(c)* _____ for me.
11. There are *(a)* _____ basic observations that
    make all empirical *(b)* _____ possible. Recite
    these observations.
12. Everything is *(a)* _____ exactly as it
    (b) _____ should be, even though it's
    (c) _____ what I *(d)* _____ to see;
    but I'm not *(e)* _____; that's why I can't get
    what I want merely by *(f)* _____ or wanting it.
    Just like all human beings, I have to *(g)* _____
    what's objectively *(h)* _____ before I can get
    the *(i)* _____ I want.
13. Why should a losing team in a hard-fought game still lose
    the game?
14. Define "being forced" to do things. When and how does it
    happen?

15. The main cause of TGIF syndrome is incorrectly calling the
    (a) _____ to work being (b) _____
    to work.
16. Name three healthy reasons for admitting that you choose
    your actions.
17. Describe three instantly helpful facts in this chapter that you
    remember.
18. To feel better emotionally without alcohol, other drugs, or
    brain damage, I must (a) _____ and
    (b) _____ better.
19. If I'm neither (a) _____ nor
    (b) _____, I'm describing my personal
    (c) _____ when I think or talk.
20. Any rational or irrational idea people believe will always be
    (a) _____ for them and (b) _____
    for their (c) _____ and other life
    (d) _____ of the moment.

Answers appear in Appendix II.

CHAPTER 12

Guaranteeing Your Success in Coping Better

Instantly Helpful Insights

The behavioral prescriptions in this book are proven formulas for coping better. But anyone can unwittingly make these proven formulas fail. Here's the best way to guarantee your success in using any proven formula. Make sure that you are not unwittingly working against yourself. That's what this chapter helps you do, to make sure that you are not unwittingly working against yourself.

Many people read at least one self-help book a year but still don't make the self-improvements they desire. Why? My research shows that these people are victims of one or more of the Common Sense Beliefs (CSB) discussed in this chapter. These CSB's do *not* occur here in their numbered order in YUPI. Instead, the CSB's occur here in the order that most people initially use them to defend their current poor coping habits. That's why I have listed them as "First Main Cause of Poor Coping, Second Main Cause . . . ," etc.

Under each CSB you will find obvious relevant facts and a rational check of it using the Five Rational Questions. They are the same questions you are to use when you want to see how rational any idea is, so pay particular attention to the following routine for rationally checking ideas, and for writing your REI scripts.

First, write the idea to be checked.

Second, give an honest yes or no answer to each of the Five

Rational Questions about that idea. Also state the reason for your answer.

Third, if you can't give at least three honest yes answers plus their reasons for an idea, replace it immediately. But make sure your replacement has these two features: (1) You believe the new idea. (2) You are willing to use that new idea—that is, you are willing to think and react to it with logical physical actions in every situation when you formerly reacted to the old idea—even if you don't yet have the logical emotional feelings for that new idea.

Fourth, put your new rational idea into one or two short sentences from your everyday self-talks; then use those sentences as your REI script and in your everyday self-counseling.

The CSB's described in this chapter are very powerful yet subtle barriers to success in coping best. That's why in the discussion of each, I have included often ignored but obvious facts about them. I have also listed the most common NII's and YUPI items that may overlap or interlock with those CSB's and thereby interfere with you using the prescribed REI scripts to erase and replace them.

IMPORTANT FACTS

Overlapping YUPI items sometimes create cognitive-emotive dissonance, thereby making REI scripts initially "feel wrong." This is the best coping strategy for that event. Turn to the discussion of the suspected YUPI item; carefully read it and copy its REI script on an index card; then alternate that REI script with the other overlapping one for five (instead of three) consecutive days; then go on to the next CSB discussed in this chapter.

For most people, most of the time, the prescribed REI scripts will give the best coping results for the psychoemotional pollutants they accompany. But no REI script is perfect for everyone all of the time, so rewrite any REI script that does not seem to fit your unique situation. Just make sure that your new REI script deserves three or more of your honest yes answers to the Five Rational Questions (see Chapter 1).

Regardless of how you score the CSB's in this chapter, do REI with them as instructed above and in Chapter 9. These CSB's items are so subtle in their negative influence that low scores on them are often misleading.

Special Vocabulary for Chapter 12

"Brain" thinking. Rejecting or accepting ideas or proposed actions mainly on the basis of objectively supportable thoughts about them.

Emotionally naive. Refers to people who don't see or believe that their own beliefs and attitudes are the only "he's," "she's," "It's," and "they's" that can cause sane, intelligent people's emotional feelings.

Gut thinking. Rejecting or accepting ideas or proposed actions solely on the basis of how those ideas or actions feel when the person uses them.

Important Questions Answered in Chapter 12

1. How does confusion about natural and normal behaviors prevent people from improving their emotional control?
2. What does the phrase "my natural and normal reactions" really tell you about your behaviors?
3. Can people's natural and normal behaviors sometimes be unhealthy and irrational for them?
4. What do your gut feelings really tell you about an idea or action?
5. How can sane, intelligent people really feel that an idea or proposed action is right when it's actually both wrong and self-defeating?
6. Are the people described in item #5 just undiagnosed crazy people?
7. What is the Irrational Gooney Bird Syndrome?
8. Do you have the Irrational Gooney Bird Syndrome?
9. What is the evidence that you don't have the Irrational Gooney Bird Syndrome with reference to your persistent problem?

First Main Cause of Poor Coping

CSB #21: I believe it's natural and normal to be upset when things that are really important to me don't go the way they should.*

*To get the most from this discussion, first read NII #1 in Chapter 10.

OBVIOUS RELEVANT FACTS

When people begin to cope better with their usually undesirable events, they feel less emotionally miserable; however, feeling less miserable in those situations is then unnatural and abnormal for them. But is that fact bad or unfortunate? No, no, no! In these cases, such people's most natural and normal emotions are miserable and undesirable. But true believers in CSB #21 act as if they believe that all natural and normal behaviors are good for them, and all unnatural and abnormal behaviors are bad for them. Let's see what the Five Rational Questions show about CSB #21.

THE FIVE RATIONAL QUESTIONS FOR CSB #21

RQ #1: Is CSB #21 based on obvious fact? No. As explained in NII #1, (Chapter 10), things always go the way they should go. True believers in CSB #21 either don't know, or they ignore that fact as well as the next one.

When behaviors are normal and natural, that only means that the people have practiced the behaviors enough to make them habitual. That's why normal and natural behaviors occur with minimal conscious effort and thought. But normal and natural behaviors can be and often are unhealthy or bad for people. The following example clearly shows that fact.

What is the most natural and normal behavior for a habitual chain smoker? It's smoking a cigarette during virtually every waking minute. Yet there are few more unhealthy, bad, or generally self-defeating voluntary behaviors.

RQ #2: Does CSB #21 best help me protect my life and health? No. Some natural and normal upsets are unhealthy.

RQ #3: Does CSB #21 best help me achieve my short- and long-term goals? No. True believers in CSB #21 often are so normally and naturally upset about their real and imagined disappointments in life that they neglect to pursue their goals, or refuse to pursue their goals because they are afraid that no matter what they do, "things will not go the way they should go."

RQ #4: Does CSB #21 best help me avoid my most undesirable conflicts with others? No. Other people frequently do not behave the way true believers in CSB #21 believe they should; that fact results in frequent, unwanted interpersonal conflicts.

RQ #5: Does CSB #21 best help me feel the way I want to feel without alcohol or other drugs? No.

CSB #21 is clearly irrational. To cope better, I must improve my thinking to the level of:

MY PRESCRIBED REI SCRIPT FOR CSB #21

I mentally see myself in a situation where I normally think CSB #21, but now I am sincerely thinking: The phrase "my normal behavior" means only that I have made those behaviors my usual behaviors. My "natural behavior" means only that I now have that behavior with the least amount of conscious effort and thought. But to improve my emotional control, I must be willing to be abnormally and unnaturally less emotionally miserable. Then I must continue to make myself abnormally and unnaturally less emotionally miserable, until being less emotionally miserable becomes normal and natural for me. Then, being more emotionally miserable than I want to be will have become so abnormal and unnatural for me that I'll just refuse to react that way anymore.

Author's Note: For a few people CSB #27 (see Chapter 2) is an even bigger barrier to self-help success than CSB #21. Check it out, and if you think CSB #27 applies to you, copy its REI script on an index card. Then, in your daily REI's, alternate the two REI scripts (i.e., one day use the CSB #21 script, then the next day use the CSB #27 script) for five consecutive days. Then go to CSB #16, below.

NII #3 and CSP #7, 11, and 19 and CSB's #7, 11, 22, 23, and 27 may interfere with my corrective REI's for CSB #21.

Second Main Cause of Poor Coping

CSB #16: I believe what feels right to me is the most important thing for me to consider in deciding how it's best for me to think, act, and react.

OBVIOUS RELEVANT FACTS

CSB #16 is a perfectly rational and useful belief when, but *only* when, what feels right to you deserves three or more honest yes answers to the Five Rational Questions. Remember, though, the alligator story (Chapter 4) clearly showed you that incorrect beliefs feel just as right as correct beliefs feel.

Unfortunately, true believers in CSB #16 tend to focus on what they incorrectly think they feel emotionally, when it would be better for them to focus on what they rationally think. To fully understand this, carefully read on about *the common misuse of the word feel*.

People commonly say "I feel" when the reality is they are naively describing their personal beliefs. Now let's look at the main reason this popular but insidious habit creates problems. *It instantly kills motivation for objective thinking.*

Merely by innocently replacing your "I think . . . " or "I believe . . . " with "I feel . . . " you instantly make totally irrational beliefs appear to you to be objective facts, if not divine revelations. Then the Five Rational Questions seem to be unnecessary, if not ludicrous. Virtually all normal Americans (even well-educated scientists) naively play that self-deceptive trick on themselves. Fortunately, they stop tricking themselves as soon as they accept the following medical facts.

THE NATURE OF GENUINE FEELINGS

Genuine human feelings of any type are objective, neurophysiological realities; they are also their own proof. That's why they don't need any other supporting or confirming evidence: They either exist or they don't. That's why, before people learn their emotional A,B,C's, the idea of checking the objective validity or rational basis of what they say they feel seems illogical, if not stupid. So partly in defense of their sense of logic and intelligence, people resist questioning the ideas they say they feel.

Such attitudes are valid for *physical* feelings. "If something feels hot or cold or wet to you, it's only because it most probably is hot, cold, or wet." But here's an important fact that poorly coping people usually ignore: *Emotional feelings do not work like physical feelings.*

The alligator story in Chapter 4 clearly showed that the sincere statement "I feel that there are alligators in this lake" may have absolutely nothing to do with the reality of alligators being in the lake. You may well be describing only the fearful emotional feelings you believe people should feel when they really are sharing a lake with alligators. But if no alligators are there, the fearful emotion would be inappropriate for the reality; the associated physical behavior would most likely be inappropriate, too.

A GOOD TEST TO REVEAL IDEAS MISLABELED AS FEELINGS

If you can replace the word *feel* with the words *think* or *believe* and your statement *keeps the same meaning*, then your statement describes only your personal opinion—and not a genuine feeling. For example, "I feel hot, cold, love, hate," etc., describe genuine feelings. If we replace *feel* with *think*: "I think hot or I believe love, cold, hate," etc., the meaning changes, if not disappears completely. But "I feel that you are taking advantage of me" does *not* describe a genuine feeling. That's why "I think or believe that you are taking advantage of me" expresses the same idea and meaning.

Why is that test helpful? People are most likely to check the rationality of opinions and beliefs before acting on them only if they admit: "These are personal opinions or beliefs." People who freely make that admission also use the word *feel* only to describe genuine one-word feelings. The opposite is true for people who say "I feel" when "I think or believe" is the objective reality.

That's why "I just didn't feel that it was right for me" is the most popular swan song of people who cope poorly.

IMPORTANT FACTS TO REMEMBER

The names of genuine or real feelings (both physical and emotional) almost all are one-word nouns and adjectives that label only human sensations.

"I feel wet, I feel hate, I feel love, I feel cold, I feel depressed," etc., are genuine or real feelings. But "I feel *that* I'm wet, I feel *that* he hates me," etc., are *not* statements of feelings.* They are statements of beliefs or opinions mislabeled as feelings. Those statements really mean: "I feel emotionally the way I probably would feel if what I think I feel accurately fitted the objective reality." Next is a real-life example of how misuse of the word *feel* prevented potentially helpful communication between good friends.

Jack was an air force buddy of mine who was about to go into a very inappropriate marriage; inappropriate, that is, based on the

---

*Whether or not people say "I feel that," if a *that* is only implied, the statement still describes a belief instead of a feeling.

known facts about the behavioral tendencies and strong preferences of both parties. Unfortunately, Willie (our other buddy) and I tried to help Jack make our insight; but we failed and lost him as a buddy for a year.*

JACK: "But I really feel that this is the right thing for me to do."

ME: "But what's the evidence that it's the right thing?"

WILLIE: "Yeah, you know they say that love sometimes makes you act crazy. How do you know that this is the right thing to do?"

JACK: "My feelings tell me so. If this thing were really wrong, I don't see how I could feel so right about it. Besides, it would be crazy for me to feel this right if it were really wrong. Do you think I'm crazy? I assure you that I'm not. I've only felt this way once before, and I let my mother talk me out of it. But I've regretted it ever since because I really feel that that was the biggest mistake I ever made. So I'll be damned if I'm going that route again."

ME: "But we just think that . . . "

JACK: "Look, I really feel that it's none of you guys' damn business."

WILLIE: "I see your point, and you are right. But we just felt that, you know—well, I'm sorry we brought it up, too."

ME: "Yeah, me too. And I'm really sorry you think that we stepped out of line."

Rationally speaking, Jack's statements were excellent examples of the intelligent-sounding noises that direct the behavior of true believers in CSB #16. If he had used brain thinking instead of gut thinking, he probably would have avoided an unhappy marriage and costly divorce.

GUT THINKING VERSUS BRAIN THINKING

Brain thinking means rejecting or accepting ideas or proposed actions mainly on the basis of objectively supportable thoughts. It's irrelevant how the person *feels* about those ideas or actions. Gut thinking means rejecting or accepting ideas or proposed actions

---

*The marriage didn't even last that long. This happened before I had learned my emotional A,B,C's and had created Rational Self-Counseling. So my buddies and I were about as emotionally naive as most well-educated people.

mainly on the basis of how those ideas or actions *feel* to the person when he or she thinks them or acts them out.

The main problem with gut thinking is that it prevents people from learning any new facts or actions that conflict with their old mistaken beliefs. Anything new that conflicts with an old belief *always* feels wrong, at least at first. But gut thinking forces people to reject anything that feels wrong. That's why gut thinking gives people the Irrational Gooney Bird Syndrome.

Irrational Gooney Birds fly backward. They are much more interested in where they have been than in where they are going. So-called gut feelings are just emotional reactions triggered by people's silent attitudes. Attitudes always reflect past experiences; they, therefore, tell people only where they have been psychoemotionally—not where they are going.

Gut thinking is, however, not all bad. In fact, rational gut thinking is what enables people to get through the day correctly with the least amount of conscious effort. Why? Because gut thinking tells people whether or not they are experiencing something new and different versus their habitual experiences. When everything looks, sounds, and feels the same old way, people usually have their same old life experiences. Now let's take a close look at *where gut feelings of right and wrong come from.*

"Feeling right" means people are reacting with their usual emotions to their personal beliefs or attitudes about familiar events. That's both logical and predictable. Sane, intelligent people do not *knowingly* hold beliefs or attitudes that they are convinced are wrong. Understandably, then, people apply the description "feels right" to all the emotions their beliefs and attitudes trigger. But, unfortunately, people use the label "feels wrong" for all the new emotional feelings triggered by any idea or action that conflicts with their personal beliefs or attitudes about familiar events.

The logic of gut feelings is: If "it" (an idea or action) feels wrong, "it" must be wrong and I should ignore "it" even though it may well be correct. The opposite logic applies when an idea or action feels right. Next is my favorite well-known example of how gut logic adversely influences people's everyday lives.

Fortunately, the laughter and refusal of these sane, intelligent people to accept that new fact did not change the shape of the earth one iota. All their gut thinking and logic did was unnecessarily delay the discovery of the new world. As stated earlier, CSB #16 is: I believe that what feels right to me is the most important thing for me to consider in deciding how it's best for me to think act and react.

THE RATIONAL QUESTIONS FOR CSB #16

RQ #1: Is CSB #16 based on obvious fact? No. The most important things for me to consider in my self-control are the obvious facts of my situation and what's rational for me in relation to them.

RQ #2: Does CSB #16 best help me to protect my life and health? No. I sometimes feel angry enough to behave in self-defeatingly dangerous ways.

RQ #3: Does CSB #16 best help me achieve my short- and long-term goals? No, because my emotional feelings are *no more reliable* than my attitudes and beliefs that trigger them. Also, people who control themselves primarily with their emotional feelings give themselves the Irrational Gooney Bird Syndrome.

RQ #4: Does CSB #16 best help me avoid my most undesirable conflicts with others? No. More often than not, blindly accepting and acting on my real negative feelings about other people create more undesirable conflicts than these actions help me avoid.

RQ #5: Does CSB #16 best help me feel the emotions I want to feel without alcohol or other drugs? No. People who score higher than 2 on CSB #16 often abuse alcohol and other drugs as a way of controlling their intensely negative feelings.

CSB #16 is clearly irrational. To cope better, I must improve my thinking to the level of:

MY PRESCRIBED REI SCRIPT FOR CSB #16

I now mentally see myself in a situation where I normally think CSB #16, but I sincerely think: My rational beliefs and attitudes are much more reliable for my self-control than my emotional feelings are. Therefore, when deciding how it's best for me to act or react, I shall ignore my gut thinking and control myself with my rational brain thinking, as Mother Nature seems to have intended.

CSP's #7, 11, 12, 19, 22, and 24 and CSB's #22, 23, 27, and 28 may interfere with my corrective REI's for CSB #16.

Memory Aid Questions for Chapter 12

1. Do you know two CSB's that prevent people from making self-improvements? Yes or No. If not, review them.
2. Write on index cards the two REI scripts for the CSB's in question #1.
3. The prescribed REI scripts are perfect for everybody all the time. True or False?
4. The best routine for (a) _____ checking an idea has (b) _____ parts.
5. What if your present idea checks out to be rational?
6. Your natural and normal behaviors are always the best for you and you should not change them. True or False?
7. What does the phrase, "my natural and normal behavior" really mean?
8. Your gut feelings do *not* give you more useful information than you can usually get by thinking rationally. True or False?
9. What do your gut feelings tell you?
10. If an idea or action really "feels right," then it's best to act on it, even though your rational check says the idea or action is irrational. True or False?
11. Having the (a) _____ Gooney Bird (b) _____ means that you are what?
12. What's the "good news" about gut thinking?
13. When in doubt, which is almost always the best to follow: (a) Your gut feelings or (b) your rational brain thinking?

Answers appear in Appendix II.

CHAPTER 13

The Value of Rational Rhetoric

Instantly Helpful Insights

The emphasis in Chapter 12 was on erasing the first two common sense beliefs that cause poor coping. Chapter 13 continues that emphasis for five other CSB's. But the discussions will also focus on the logic and value of using rational rhetoric, that is, using everyday words in the most objectively precise as well as rational way possible.

Important Questions Answered in Chapter 13

1. If people are talking about themselves, when are they most likely to switch from "I" to "you" statements?
2. How do the people in item #1 usually feel about themselves?
3. What happens psychologically when people sincerely refer to themselves as "you"?
4. What are the basic requirements for being an effective advice-giver?
5. Why is it that people in question #3 rarely improve their self-control?
6. Can your miserable past make you have personal problems now? If yes, how?
7. The people who answer yes to question #6 have usually made what decision?
8. Do the people in question #7 enjoy feeling miserable?
9. What's the best thing to do about a miserable past?
10. How can you objectively choose to have a happy day every day?

Third Main Cause of Poor Coping

CSB #32: I believe that there are universal standards of right and wrong that everybody should follow regardless of their personal feelings about them.

WHO IS RIGHT AND WHO IS WRONG

Over three thousand years ago behavioral scientists pointed out: "Every way of people is right in their own eyes" (*Proverbs*: 21:2). Therefore, everyone is right until they themselves believe they are wrong. Obviously then, there can't ever be universal standards of right and wrong. There can be only the arbitrary rules and ideas governments, groups, and individuals accept and live by.

MY PRESCRIBED REI SCRIPT FOR CSB #32

I now mentally see myself in a situation where I normally think CSB #32, but I am sincerely thinking: Every honest person is right in his or her own mind. So when others and I honestly disagree, I shall remember that we are all right; but that's irrelevant when neither of us is getting what we want. That's why I shall keep myself rationally calm naturally and look for ideas that are rational for them *and* for me. If I fail, I shall either rationally choose to go along or rationally forget about the situation and get on with my life.

CSP's #8, 12, 13, 18, 19, 20, and 24 may interfere with my REI's for CSB #32.

Fourth Main Cause of Poor Coping

CSB #9: I believe there is me and another "real" me.

OBVIOUS RELEVANT FACTS

True believers in CSB #9 usually have a severe self-dislike, if not a passionate self-hate. They believe their "real" selves have some well-hidden despicable traits that can't be changed. To get the approval of others, these true believers pretend to have popular personality traits and personal values that they don't really have. That's how they hide their imagined despicable traits and thereby try to avoid other people's hate and rejection. Now let's see how CSB #9 leads these people to self-help failure.

CSB #9 makes it appear logical to refer to oneself as "you" instead of "I." Usually these true believers flip into "you" self-references when they think about their unwanted behaviors or imagined despicable traits.* Next are excerpts from an interview with a student who clearly demonstrated the negative results "you" self-references cause true believers in CSB #9. This student was receiving counseling because of his depression about his failing grades in college. Notice when he switched from "I" to "you."

ME: "Tell me exactly what happened last semester."

S: "I started off the first six weeks with good intentions to study. I told myself that I was not going to goof off and fall behind in anything. And I followed through on that.

"The first six weeks I went directly to my room after class and I hit the books hard and heavy. I really felt great, especially about the good grades I got. But then the second six weeks rolled around; and *you* get to missing *your* friends. You see, I hadn't even been stopping by the Student Union for beers like I used to, or any of that stuff; I had just been going to class and back to my dorm and hitting the books and that was it. So then *you* start feeling a little guilty about neglecting *your* friends and missing out on all the real fun of being in college; so *you* naturally start dropping by the Student Union once in a while for a cup of coffee and a little rapping with *your* friends."

---

*It's irrelevant that almost "everybody" does that sometimes. In the minds and brains of superreactive people, CSB #9 causes self-help failure. And remember, even when almost "everyone" believed the world was flat, that was still a self-defeating belief for sailors to have.

Author's Note: Did you notice that when the student was describing his desirable rational behavior, he said, "I"? But when he was describing the undesirable irrational behavior that produced his failing grades he said "you"? That's typical of people who are trying to disown their self-defeating behaviors. The student continued:

S: "After rapping for a while *you* naturally feel a little hungry so *you* order a sandwich; but *you* think: I have to go right after the sandwich, and I'm about to go; but then one of *your* friends offers *you* a beer and *you* take it just to be friendly; but then there's another one, and by that time *you* are really involved in some great conversation and *you* don't feel much like studying anyway. So *you* stay.

"But *you* think: I'm going to get up early in the morning and study and make up for the time that I didn't study tonight. But the next day, *you* wake up late, *you've* got a headache, and *you* realize that *you* had a little more beer than *you* should have; that's why *you* forgot to set *your* clock and why *you* slept through *your* first class.

Then *you* rush off to *your* next class, but *you* are not prepared and *you* don't get much out of it.

"So *you* start feeling bad about that; and things like that just keep on happening to *you* more and more each week until the first thing *you* know, *your* study schedule is gone out the window; but *your* work is still piling up on *you*, and *you* finally see that there's just no way that *you* can possibly catch up before the final exam. So *you* start feeling anxious and then *you* get depressed. So then *you're* too depressed to study or anything. That kept up until I finally said: '*Max*, *you* dumb ass, *you* did it again! When will *you* get it through *your* head that *you* have to plan *your* work and then work *your* plan? Now get *your* lazy ass in gear and go over to Student Counseling and get some help with this damn depression. Then get a medical excuse to get I's instead of F's and then turn them into A's and B's next semester.' And so here I am. I want you all to give me a little help in getting my act together."

THE SELF-DEFEATING DYNAMICS OF THE "I" TO "YOU" SWITCH

What happens psychologically when people sincerely refer to themselves with the second person "you"? They experience themselves as if they are two people occupying the same body at the same time; it seems as if there's a rational, responsible "I-self" and an irrational, irresponsible "you-self." Typically, the imaginary rational I-self angrily lectures the imaginary irrational you-self about his or her undesirable behavior. But only rarely does self-improvement occur. The following is one of this student's angry self-lectures, written at my request.

He wrote: "*You've* got to stop being so damn lazy!!! When are *you* going to learn to say 'no' to *your* crazy beer-slopping friends; *you've* got to make up *your* mind to cut out the crap and get *your* act together. *You* can't go on filling *your* mind with this Bull!!! *You're* so damn stupid; *you're* just a bum, a dumb nobody. *You* had better get off it or *you'll* be kicked out of school for sure. Damn! I sure hate like hell to have to depend on *you*."

After such an angry lecture, the imaginary rational I-self usually sits back and patiently waits for the irrational you-self to start behaving more responsibly. But, of course, there *is no* real irrational you-self to take the rational I-self's advice. And the real I-self can't take his or her own advice. Why not? Because if he or she did that, it would seem to prove that the imaginary rational I-self is just as irrational and, therefore, as bad off as the imaginary irrational you-self who has just been lectured.

Normally, for effective advice-giving to occur, one of these two necessary (but not sufficient) conditions must exist: *(1)* the advisors about the problem either have avoided having the problem in spite of similar life experiences to those of the advisee; or *(2)* the advisors freely admit that they either had or now have the problem, but they show obvious objective evidence of having either solved the problem or of coping in the best possible way with it. In addition, the advice of the second type of advisors must be limited to personal descriptions of how they either did or are now successfully applying their advice to themselves. Otherwise the advisors' credibility will be too low for them to appropriately influence the advisees. Those basic conditions apply even when *the advisor and advisee are the same person.*

None of those conditions apply to true believers in CSB #9. The real person is both the imaginary I-self and you-self. But in their you-self lectures these true believers identify only with their imaginary rational I-selves. However, the imaginary I-selves don't have the problem, and, therefore, don't need to change. By identifying with the I-self it seems to the real person that he or she does not need to change either; so neither makes any behavioral changes. Instead, they both patiently wait for the you-self to change him or herself. The only problem is that imaginary you-selves do not make behavioral changes, so only rarely does any behavioral improvement occur at all.

There is one other reason the real person refuses to take the advice that the imaginary I-self gives to the imaginary irrational you-self. If the real person were to take the imaginary I-self's advice, that would solve the problem without the imaginary irrational you-self doing anything. That event would make the angry imaginary I-self's lectures seem to have been irrelevant, if not stupid, instead of insightful and smart. In part, therefore, to protect their self-images of being smart, insightful people, these true believers and their imaginary I-selves have to patiently wait for the imaginary irrational you-selves to take the advice in the you-self lectures. But, as I pointed out earlier, imaginary people don't take real people's advice.

THE RATIONAL QUESTIONS FOR CSB #9

RQ #1. Is CSB #9 based on obvious fact? No. There is only one of each individual; that fact never changes regardless of how many different ways people refer to themselves.

RQ #2. Does CSB #9 best help me protect my life and health? No. True believers in CSB #9 often have irrational depressions that lead to suicidal gestures and often to suicide.

RQ #3. Does CSB #9 best help me achieve my short- and long-term goals in life? No. Although true believers in CSB #9 angrily lecture themselves, they rarely achieve their desired self-improvements.

RQ #4. Does CSB #9 best help me avoid my most undesirable conflicts with others? No. True believers in CSB #9 usually perform poorly and, therefore, often disappoint other people. That behavior frequently causes undesirable conflicts with those other people.

RQ #5. Does CSB #9 best help me feel the emotions I want to feel without alcohol or other drugs? No. CSB #9 often causes people to abuse alcohol and other legal and illegal drugs in their attempts to feel better emotionally without thinking better.

CSB #9 is clearly irrational. To cope better I must improve my thinking to the level of:

MY PRESCRIBED REI SCRIPT FOR CSB #9

I now mentally see myself in a situation where I normally think CSB #9, but I am sincerely thinking: There is only one of me; therefore, I shall always refer to myself using only the objectively correct "I." I shall rationally own up to all of my undesirable behaviors; but I shall rationally refuse to make myself feel any worse emotionally about them than actually helps me cope better with them then and in the future.

NII #3; CSP #1, CSB #1, 14, and 10 may interfere with my corrective REI's for CSB #9.

Fifth Main Cause of Poor Coping

CSB #18: I believe that it's my regrettable past that is causing me my personal problems now.

OBVIOUS RELEVANT FACTS

True believers in CSB #18 have committed themselves (often without realizing it) to living as miserably as they possibly can and still appear to be sane. That's why they resist taking obvious rational steps to reduce or eliminate their unhappiness. Instead they incessantly "analyze" and redescribe how and who—parents, spouses, employers, friends, enemies, etc.—made their past lives miserable.

That never-ending mental practice in reliving their miserable past keeps these people highly skilled in making themselves instantly and often continually miserable in the present. But these people blame their present emotional misery on their past. That maneuver keeps them from seriously considering self-improvement. Instead they repeatedly explain: "I'm telling the truth. Those people actually did do those terrible things to me! So why should I have to be the one to change? They shouldn't have treated me that way. They should have . . . " Those irrational *shoulds* and *shouldn'ts* keep these people blind to this obvious fact: *They, themselves are the only ones who can change the influence their miserable pasts have on them now.*

Is it that these people just enjoy being miserable? No. These are sane, intelligent people; sane, intelligent people *do not* enjoy being miserable; it's just that these people really believe in CSB #18. And healthy brains don't care what self-defeating ideas people believe. Healthy brains just immediately convert people's beliefs into their real-life experiences of the moment, just as Mother Nature programmed them to do. That biological programming is *also* why doing REI with the prescribed REI script for CSB #18 quickly erases and replaces CSB #18 with natural happiness and better coping skills. But first, let's do the rational check of CSB #18.

THE RATIONAL QUESTIONS FOR CSB #18

RQ #1: Is CSB #18 based on obvious fact? No. Every person's past is just that, *past*, over and done. That's why my past can affect me now only through my memory of it. But I control my memory; that's why I decide which of my memories I focus on. Merely by ignoring my regrettable past I can easily and quickly free myself from it.

RQ #2: Does CSB #18 best help me protect my life and health? No. People who score higher than 2 on CSB #18 are often victims of suicidal depression.

RQ #3: Does CSB #18 best help me achieve my short- and long-term goals in life? No, not unless I have the short- and long-term goals of living as miserably as possible.

RQ #4: Does CSB #18 best help avoid my most undesirable conflicts with others? No. Victims of CSB #18 usually engage in a continuous mental and actual conflict with the real and imagined culprits associated with their miserable past experiences.

RQ #5: Does CSB #18 best help me feel the emotions I want to feel without alcohol or other drugs? No. Honestly scoring three or more on CSB #18 can virtually ensure a life of continuous unwanted emotional misery.

CSB #18 is clearly irrational. To cope better, I must improve my thinking to the level of:

MY PRESCRIBED REI SCRIPT FOR CSB #18

I now mentally see myself in a situation where I normally think CSB #18, but I am sincerely thinking: My past affects me now only through my memories of it. But I control my memories. And it's just as easy to remember my pleasant past as it is to remember my unpleasant past. But what if I don't have a happy past that's worth remembering? Then the best thing for me to do is rewrite my past to my satisfaction. How? Easily. If I just live my life today as happily as I can, tomorrow I will have an instant, happier past that I can remember and enjoy anytime I choose to do so.

My past of only one day is just as real, genuine, and appropriate for me to remember and enjoy as my past of last month, last year, or of many decades ago. And if I live my life each day as happily as I can, I will be so busy enjoying myself that I won't have time to remember my most recent past, even though it will be my happiest past. But that's all right. My past never gets tired of waiting; it always will be there for me to remember, as miserably or as happily as I desire. The choice is mine; that's why today I choose to have a happier day.*

CSP's #1, 14, 15 and CSB #28 may interfere with my corrective REI's for CSB #18.

The next two CSB's are so obviously irrational that I omitted the rational checks, but the prescribed REI script still accompanies each. For your own self-training, though, it's still a good idea to do your own rational check of each CSB.

---

*Excerpted with permission from audiotape #3 in the "Create Your Own Happiness" Kit, by Maxie C. Maultsby, Jr., M.D.

Sixth Main Cause of Poor Coping

CSB #5: I believe that if I act differently from my usual self, I'll be a phony person and I hate phonies.

MY PRESCRIBED REI SCRIPT FOR CSB #5

I now mentally see myself in a situation where I normally think CSB #5, but I am sincerely thinking: The only phony people are mannequins; but I can't ever be a mannequin; so it's stupid to call myself a phony. What I have been naively calling being phony was actually the unavoidable cognitive-emotive dissonance everybody feels when they first start acting and thinking better. But to learn the better coping skill that I desire, I have to ignore my odd, or *seemingly* phony, gut feelings and continually practice thinking and acting better until that better behavior becomes habitual; that is, until I automatically have the logical emotional feelings for my better new thoughts and actions. But, no matter how many of my usual behaviors that I change for the better, or to what extent I change them, I still will be my real self with better personal behaviors.

The following CSP's may interfere with my corrective REI's for CSB #5: CSP's #7, 14, and 15.

Seventh Main Cause of Poor Coping

CSB #28: I believe that if I make an honest effort to do something and still fail at it, that means that I can't do it, or it just was not meant for me to have that success.

MY PRESCRIBED REI SCRIPT FOR CSB #28

I now mentally see myself in a situation where I normally think CSB #28, but I am sincerely thinking: Any task worth doing at all is always worth my honest effort. But to succeed at anything, I must make sure that my honest effort fits with what objectively seems likely to be effective. Otherwise, my honest effort may turn out to be an honest waste of time. In addition to always picturing myself making only those kinds of efforts, at every opportunity I shall actually act out my REI's in real life.

CSP's #6, 11, 14, 15, and 20 may interfere with my corrective REI's for CSB #28.

Memory Aid Questions for Chapter 13

1. For your psychoemotional pollutants that are not in YUPI, you are to use the *(a)* _____ check and the *(b)*_____ *(c)* _____ to analyze your problem-related *(d)*_____.
2. After the action in item #1, you are to write your own _____ script.
3. Finally you are to do *(a)* _____ REI's until you *(b)* _____ the *(c)* _____ coping *(d)* _____ you desire.
4. Doing daily REI's can decrease the undesirable influences of many different YUPI items at the same time. True or False?
5. To get the better coping skills that I desire, I must do daily *(a)* _____ and real *(b)*_____; *(c)* _____ long *(d)* _____ to *(e)* _____ my *(f)* _____ coping skills.
6. When people don't want to take personal *(a)* _____ for their undesirable behaviors, they are likely to refer to themselves using *(b)* _____ instead of *(c)*_____.
7. When people sincerely use "you" to describe their own hated behaviors, they get the *(a)* _____ that there are *(b)* _____ of them, an *(c)* _____ self and a *(d)* _____ self.
8. List the basic conditions for being an effective advice-giver.
9. People who lecture themselves using "you" instead of "I" *(a)* _____ improve their *(b)*_____.
10. Why is the answer to item #9 as it is?
11. How can you choose to have a happy day today and every day?

Answers appear in Appendix II.

SECTION V

Mini-Encyclopedias of Common Problems and Prescriptions for Coping Better with Absolutely Anything at Anytime

CHAPTER 14: **Your Instant Emotional Checkup**—An index of the most common emotional, general life, and medical problems that poor coping causes.

CHAPTER 15: **Prescriptions for Coping Better with Common Sense Perceptions (CSP's)**—A listing of all the common sense perceptions in Your Unhappiness Potential Inventory and the best coping prescriptions for them.

CHAPTER 16: **Prescriptions for Coping Better with Common Sense Beliefs (CSB's)**—A listing of all the common sense beliefs and the best coping prescriptions for them.

I hope that you have been reading this book as suggested. If you have, you have already reduced or eliminated much of the negative influence many YUPI items have had on your coping ability. Therefore, the self-help prescriptions in this section will most quickly give you the better coping skills you desire.

The chapters in this section have different formats, roles in your better coping efforts and a different reading routines from the other chapters. To benefit most from those differences, before you go to Chapter 14, do these two things: (1) Review each NII and YUPI items in Chapters 10 through 13. (2) Copy on index cards the REI script of all items that you believe still deserve a score of 3 or more. Then systematically repeat the three-day REI routine on each such items until you can honestly score it at 2 or less.

Read Chapter 14 straight through, as you did Chapters 1 through 13. But read Chapters 15 and 16 selectively, as described in "Your First Option," in the section "Your Other Two Options" at the end of Chapter 14.

Your Instant Emotional Checkup

Instantly Helpful Insights

If you are like most normal people, you sometimes wonder: Do I really have a problem that I just refuse to admit; or am I just too particular? The following fact will enable you to answer that question with confidence.

Any life event becomes a personal problem for everybody the instant they get more upset about it than actually helps them cope better with it.

Your Instant Emotional Checkup is a three-part list of common problem in daily living. Part A is a list of common emotional problems with numbers referring to their prescribed best REI scripts. Part B is a short list of common life problems. Special self-help information and instructions for all of them appear at the end of the list. Part C is a list of psychosomatic illnesses. Again, special self-help information and instructions for all of them appear at the end of the list.

Special Vocabulary for Chapter 14

Psychosomatic Illness. Any medical problem thought to be mainly caused by or made worse by emotional distress. Ideal treatment for psychosomatic illness consists of medical treatment and psychotherapy being given at the same time. The illness itself, however, is still a medical problem, so a physician needs to be involved as long as medical symptoms exist.

What to Do Now

Thoughtfully read the following list of problems. As you read, write on an index card (in the order of their troublesomeness for you) any problems with which you may want to start coping better immediately. You will find additional instruction at the end of the list.

What if you don't have or don't want to work on any of the three lists of problems? Then you can exercise one of "Your Other Two Options," which appear at the end of this chapter.

PART A: COMMON EMOTIONAL PROBLEMS

1. Anger (excessive amounts): NII's #1 and 2; CSB #32
2. Anxiety (excessive amounts): CSP's #16 and 21; CSB's #7 and 19
3. Being used: CSP's #8 and 10; CSB's #26 and 32
4. Burnout: NII's #1–5; CSP's #18, 19, and 20; CSB #32
5. Depression: NII's #1–5; CSP's #1, 4, 5, 6, 7; CSB's #1, 4, 13, 14, 31, 33, and 35
6. Disliking self: CSP's #1, 4, 6, 7; CSB's #13, 31, 33, and 35
7. Emotional blackmail: CSB's #30 and 34
8. Emotional dependency needs (inadequately met): CSP #13; CSB's #17, 29, 30, 34, and 35
9. Fair lover's fights (too many of them): CSP's #18, 19, and 20; CSB's #24, 25, 30, 32, and 35
10. Fear of being accepted—see lover's fair fights
11. Feeling as if others are more important to you than you are: CSP #22; CSB's #17, 29, 36, and 35
12. Feeling as if there are two of you: CSP #1; CSB #9
13. Feeling as if you are being unfairly or unjustly treated: CSP's #18, 19, and 20
14. Feeling as if you are inferior as a person: CSP's #1, 4, 5, 6, 7; CSB's #1, 4, 13, 31, 33, and 35
15. Feeling different from your normal and natural self: CSB's #16, 21, and 27
16. Feeling, i.e., focusing on your feelings when it's best to focus on your thoughts: CSP #16; CSB's #16 and 19
17. Feeling unreal: CSP #7; CSB's #5 and 27
18. Irrational Gooney Bird Syndrome: CSB's #10 and 16
19. Living up to potential (not doing it): CSP #9; CSB's #4, 6, and 8
20. Luck (usually bad): CSP's #15 and 24; CSB's #18 and 36
21. Miserable past making you miserable now: CSB #18
22. Poor self-motivation—see procrastination
23. Procrastination: CSP #16; CSB's #7 and 19
24. Right versus wrong (conflicts related to it): CSB #32
25. Self-acceptance—see disliking self

26. Self-confidence (too little for success): CSP's #2 and 3; CSB #2
27. Sexual satisfaction of partners (worry about it): CSB #12
28. Stress (too much)—see anxiety and burnout
29. Trusting untrustworthy people: CSP's #21, 15, and 30
30. Wanting to hide your real self: CSB #14

SPECIAL INFORMATION AND INSTRUCTIONS FOR PART A

Any NII or YUPI items scored higher than 2 that accompanies a problem usually is a main cause of that problem. Here's the best way to work on any one of these problems.

Copy on an index card the REI scripts for your one or (not more than) two highest-scored NII or YUPI items for that problem. Then follow the three-day REI routine described in Chapter 9.

Do *not* expect to have completely solved that problem in just three days. But after three days, go on to any other one or two NII or YUPI items that are associated with that problem. Then repeat the three-day REI routine for all the NII and YUPI items for that problem, until you are coping better to your satisfaction with that problem.

If you have a psychosomatic illness, it will be all right to do this. Alternate three days of REI devoted to the unhealthy attitude associated with your psychosomatic illness with three days of REI devoted to one of the above problems. It would also be all right to alternate three days of REI on a problem in Part A with three days of REI on a problem in Part B.

PART B: COMMON LIFE PROBLEMS

1. Alcohol or other drug abuse or addiction problems
2. Business problems
3. Car problems
4. Eating problems
5. Family problems
6. Friendship problems
7. Gambling problems
8. Impulsive behavior
9. In-law problems
10. Irrational fears
11. Legal problems
12. Marital problems
13. Money problems
14. Neighbor problems
15. Obesity or less severe overweight problem
16. Parent-child problems
17. Romantic problems or roommate problems
18. School problems
19. Self-discipline problems
20. Sexual problems
21. Study problems
22. Work problems

SPECIAL INFORMATION AND INSTRUCTIONS FOR PART B

Any NII or YUPI item scored higher than 2 can cause those problems or make them worse than they otherwise would be. If you have one or more of these problems, handle its seemingly related, highly scored NII's or YUPI items as instructed in your first or second options described later in this chapter. Also, as described in Part A, if you have a psychosomatic illness, you can alternate the three-day REI routine for it with the three-day REI routine for a problem in Part B.

PART C: PSYCHOSOMATIC ILLNESSES

SPECIAL INFORMATION

People who have psychosomatic illnesses seem to have an inherited tendency to react to their personal attitudes about their stressful life events with as intense a physiologic response as they would have if their personal attitudes were themselves objective realities. That fact makes their emotional reactions feel more like physical than like emotional experiences. Understandably, then, these people tend to express their strongest stress-related attitudes in mainly physical terms instead of emotional terms.

For example, when urticaria patients face intensely stressful events, they tend to describe their experience this way: "I feel like I'm taking a beating—being knocked around, hammered on unfairly, and I'm helpless."

Like all healthy brains, the brains of urticaria patients *don't care* about the implications for their medical health that these patients' attitudes have; these healthy brains just instantly convert the unhealthy urticaria-related attitudes into the same type of unhealthy physiologic reactions that would result if the patients were actually receiving the physical beating they feel as if they are receiving.

That analysis of the psychophysiologic mechanisms in psychosomatic illness points directly to an important part of comprehensive psychosomatic treatment: It's the prescribed replacement of these patients' psychosomatically unhealthy attitudes with the opposite and therefore healthier attitudes.

Next is the list of the eighteen psychosomatic illnesses recognized by physicians who believe in the attitude-related theory of psychosomatic illness.* Accompanying each illness is the unhealthy psychosomatic attitude that seems to trigger the intense physiologic reactions associated with the illness. If you have one of these psychosomatic illnesses, copy the associated unhealthy

*There are two excellent articles on this theory of psychosomatic illness: "The Relationship of Specific Attitudes and Emotions to Certain Bodily Diseases," by W. J. Grace and D. T. Graham, published in the journal *Psychosomatic Medicine*, vol. 14 (1952); and "Specific Attitudes in Initial Interviews with Patients Having Different Psychosomatic Diseases," in *Psychosomatic Medicine*, vol. 24 (1962).

attitude on an index card. Your other instructions are at the end of the list.

1. *Acne.* Patients feel as if they are being picked on or nagged at and they want to be left alone.

2. *Bronchial asthma.* Patients feel as if they are left out in the cold and they want to shut the person or situation out; or they "feel" unloved, rejected, disapproved or shut out, and they wish not to have to deal with the person or situation; they wish to blot it or them out, not have anything to do with it or them.

3. *Constipation.* Patients feel as if they are in a situation from which nothing good can come; but they grimly keep on with it. Or, patients feel as if things will never get any better; but they have to stick with it.

4. *Duodenal ulcer.* Patients feel as if they are deprived of what is due them and they want to get even; or patients feel as if they don't get what they should, what is owed or promised to them. They want to get back at, get revenge, do to those others what they did to them.

5. *Eczema.* Patients feel as if they are being frustrated and can do nothing about it except take it out on themselves; they "feel" interfered with, blocked, prevented from doing something, and they are unable to make themselves understood.

6. *Essential hypertension.* Patients feel as if they are threatened with harm and they have to be ready for anything; or they "feel" in danger, as if anything could happen at any time from any side; so they feel as if they have to be prepared to meet all possible threats, always be on guard.

7. *Hyperthyroidism.* Patients feel as if they might lose somebody or something they love and take care of; so they feel as if they are trying to prevent that loss of a loved person or object; or, they feel as if they are trying to hold on to somebody they love and take care of, but they can't seem to really do it.

8. *Low backache.* Patients feel as if they want to run away; to walk out or get out of there, but can't.

9. *Metabolic edema.* Patients feel as if they are carrying a heavy load and they want somebody else to carry all or part of it; "feel" they have too much on their shoulders, too much responsibility; want others to take their share of it, but no one will.

10. *Migraine.* Patients feel as if they have to achieve something, then they will relax after they achieve it; or they feel as if they are driving themselves, striving, have to get things done, a goal has to be reached, then they can let down or stop the driving, but they never do stop driving.

11. *Multiple sclerosis.* Patients feel as if they are forced to undertake some kind of physical activity, especially hard work, and they do not want to do it; or they feel as if they have to work without help, have to support themselves and usually others; they don't want to do it, but they might not express their wish for help or support.

12. *Psoriasis.* Patients feel as if there is a constant gnawing at them and that they have to put up with it; they "feel" a steady boring, a constant nagging or irritation or annoyance.

13. *Raynaud's disease.* Patients feel as if they want to take hostile physical action; they want to hit or strangle, take action of any kind, do something.

14. *Regional enteritis.* Patients feel as if they are receiving something harmful and they want to get rid of it; or they feel as if they have been given something damaged or inferior; or they feel as if they have been poisoned; they want the situation to be finished, over and done with, disposed of.

15. *Rheumatoid arthritis.* Patients feel as if they are tied down and they want to get free; they "feel" restrained, restricted, confined, and they want to be able to move around.

16. *Ulcerative colitis.* Patients feel as if they are being injured and degraded and they wish they could get rid of the responsible agent; or they feel as if they are being humiliated and they want the situation to be finished, over and done with, disposed of.

17. *Urticaria.* Patients feel as if they are taking a beating and are helpless to do anyting about it; or they feel as if they are being knocked around, hammered on, being mistreated or unfairly treated.

18. *Vomiting.* Patients feel as if something wrong has happened, usually something for which they feel responsible, and wish it hadn't happened; or they feel sorry it happened, wish they could undo what has happened, wish things were the way they were before, wish they hadn't done it.

SPECIAL INSTRUCTIONS FOR PSYCHOSOMATIC ILLNESSES

If you have any of these illnesses and you are under a physician's care, please comply completely with all of your physician's advice.

In addition (and with your physician's permission), diligently take the emotional self-help prescription that's prescribed below.

If you are not under a physician's care, please consult a physician immediately. Then, with his or her permission, diligently take the emotional self-help prescription that's prescribed below.

Many psychosomatic patients wonder: What if I don't think I have the attitude that the checklist says I'm supposed to have about my stressful life events? My advice is: Remember that attitudes are the unspoken forms of personal beliefs. That's why people often have unhealthy attitudes of which they are unaware. Yet those attitudes still trigger unhealthy reactions. It's irrelevant that you may not be aware of having the listed attitude. If you have that psychosomatic illness, your body is reacting as if you do have that attitude. Here's the best way to cope with that unhealthy fact: Diligently take the following emotional self-help prescription.

Emotional self-help prescription: Memorize the opposite ideas to the unhealthy ones that are associated with your psychosomatic illness. Then every four to six hours while awake, do two to ten minutes (more if you like) of the IBFM (Instant Better Feeling Maneuver—see Chapter 3) while you repeatedly think about a stressful event that is usually associated with those unhealthy ideas. But then, think *only* the ideas that are the opposite of your illness-related attitudes.

Follow each such REI period with another two to ten minutes of REI, using a REI script that is ideally suited for coping better with that stressful event itself. Continue this daily REI routine until you have your psychosomatic illness under satisfactory control.

If you also want to work on a problem in Part A or B above, follow the special instructions under those lists of problems. And if you have an attack of psychosomatic symptoms, repeat the emotional self-help prescription over and over until you are relieved.

Now remember, a psychosomatic illness *is* a medical problem; tissue and/or organ damage has been done. Even after you have completely erased and replaced the unhealthy attitude associated with it, your medical problem will probably persist (but in less intense form) for a variable period of time. Expect that and *do not* be disappointed when it happens. With correct daily REI, however, you *can* expect quick improvement in your coping skills for the emotionally stressful events associated with your psychosomatic illness.

Your Other Two Options

Your First Option: Find in Chapter 15 or 16 and copy on an index card the REI scripts of the two most highly scored plus currently troublesome YUPI items in Chapter 2. Then use those REI scripts for daily REI as instructed above in Chapter 9. Repeat that process until you have achieved the better coping goals described in the REI scripts for all the YUPI items on which you scored higher than 2.

Your Second Option: For any personal problem that is not listed in this chapter, follow the three-day REI routine for your highest-scored YUPI items that you associate with that problem and/or for REI scripts that you write for that problem. Continue repeating the three-day REI routine on those and any other related REI scripts until you achieve your desired better coping goals.

With each option, act out your REI scripts in real life at every opportunity. Your daily REI routine plus real-life practice will most quickly give you the better coping skill that you rationally desire for absolutely anything.

Do not expect miracles, but do expect some progressive improvement in your coping power by the third day of diligent daily REI on any appropriate REI script. Still, think in terms of thirty days of daily REI as the most reasonable minimum time to get the best permanent results for your efforts. People who are not making satisfactory coping progress within thirty days may need professional help. I therefore advise them to check out that possibility.

You have now received the best of my personal, professional, and research experience. I have thoroughly enjoyed giving it to you. Now it's just a matter of daily application. Only you can do that.

CHAPTER 15

Prescriptions for Coping Better with Common Sense Perceptions (CSP's)

Instantly Helpful Insights

This chapter lists all the CSP's (Common Sense Perceptions) in YUPI. It also gives you instantly helpful facts and insights as well as specific behavioral prescriptions for daily REI's. When you take those prescriptions correctly, expect this: They will mentally and physically erase and replace your inaccurate perceptions with accurate ones that increase your coping ability and your natural happiness.

SPECIAL INSTRUCTIONS

If a prescribed REI script does not fit your unique situation, rewrite it. Then check your rewrite with the Five Rational Questions. If your rewrite proves to be rational for you, use it instead of the prescribed one.

Please *do not* read this chapter in page-by-page sequence. The chapter is a mini-encyclopedia of behavioral prescriptions for coping better with absolutely anything at anytime. You will enjoy and benefit most from this chapter if you accurately follow the instructions given in Chapter 14.

Special Vocabulary for Chapter 15

Fair. Anything two or more people agree on is fair for them; or what the people—e.g., parents, judges, etc.—with recognized enforceable authority say is fair. Synonym: Just.

Healthiest self-motivation. Getting oneself to do tasks, especially hated tasks, by sincerely thinking: I choose to do this hated task because I hope my action will produce these personal benefits. . . .

Illusion. Any inaccurate perception resulting from a misinterpretation of some objective fact. Illusions are common causes of clinical emotional distress for sane, intelligent people.

Mental-tally bookkeeping injustice collectors. People who (much more often than most otherwise similar people) both see themselves as unfairly and unjustly treated and who usually can give you a long list of both real and imagined examples of their unfair treatment.

Self-reward motivation. Getting yourself to do things mainly with hopeful thoughts about the objective personal benefits you expect to get as a consequence of your actions (the same as the healthiest self-motivation above).

Self-threat motivation. Getting yourself to do tasks mainly by sincerely thinking fear-triggering thoughts such as: I have to or I'm forced to do this to avoid the terrible or awful things that will happen if I don't.

Stupid person.   As used in this book, a human being who is objectively incapable of learning anything. It's a name or label that almost never accurately fits a human being.

AN IMPORTANT FACT TO REMEMBER

You didn't learn your CSP's in three days; and you are not going to completely erase and replace them with your REI scripts in just three days. But if you end each instance of your undesirable behavior with just *one to three minutes* of corrective REI, you will most quickly replace your undesirable behavior with your desired best coping skills.

The Common Sense Perceptions

CSP #1:   The reflection of me that I see in the mirror is not the real me.

HELPFUL FACTS AND INSIGHTS

True believers in CSP #1 equate themselves with their undesirable behaviors. If they behave stupidly, they feel as emotionally miserable as they believe stupid people should feel. Then they mislabel their miserable feeling, "feeling stupid," and conclude: "I must be stupid because I feel stupid. If I weren't stupid, I wouldn't feel this way." In reality, though, their so-called feeling stupid is a mixture of self-anger and shame.

Usually true believers in CSP #1 also have the incorrect belief that to reject their undesirable behavior they have to reject themselves. CSP #1 is the mildest form of self-rejection. Even so, it's still enough psychological self-rejection to produce chronic self-dislike and low self-motivation to improve themselves. After all, if the person they see in the mirror is not really them, there is no reason to improve the person in the mirror.

MY PRESCRIBED REI SCRIPT FOR CSP #1

I shall now mentally picture myself in a situation where I normally think CSP #1, but now I shall sincerely think: My mirrored reflection always has been, is now, and shall always be the reflection of my real self. Granted, I may have some "rotten" behaviors. But I am not ever the same as my behaviors. So I shall rationally give myself unconditional positive self-acceptance and get rid of my "rotten" behaviors as soon as possible.

HELPFUL INSIGHT

You will know that you are pursuing your behavioral goal correctly when you notice that: (1) you have stopped thinking CSP #1; (2) you immediately forgive yourself for every instance of personally undesirable behavior; and (3) you immediately take rational steps to improve or eliminate your undesirable behaviors.

The following YUPI items may interfere with my REI's on CSP #1: CSB's #1, 3, 6, 9, 16, and 31.

CSP #2: I don't have enough self-confidence.

HELPFUL FACTS AND INSIGHTS

True believers in CSP #2 act as if they believe that it would be awful or terrible if they failed at the tasks they say they don't have enough self-confidence to do. Their fear of failure is so intense that these people either (1) refuse to try at all, or (2) they give up without doing even the obvious things that could ensure their success. Then they confuse themselves with the incorrect idea that they didn't have enough self-confidence to do the task.

HELPFUL INSIGHTS ABOUT SELF-CONFIDENCE

Self-confidence is only people's beliefs about the probability of succeeding or failing at a given task. People always have a belief about that; that belief is their self-confidence, and it's always enough for their sincere estimate of their probable success or failure at that time.

When true believers in CSP #2 say: "I don't have enough self-confidence," they really mean: "I have so much confidence that I shall fail that I refuse to imagine myself doing the things that I know could ensure my success.

MY PRESCRIBED REI SCRIPT FOR CSB #2

I shall now mentally picture myself in a situation where I normally think CSP #2, but I shall now sincerely think: I shall calmly do the proven, effective things necessary to succeed at this task. Then, the only way I can fail will be because of unforeseeable events that no one could have avoided. Starting today, I shall keep myself calm with the Instant Better Feeling Maneuver while I mentally picture myself doing only the things that normally produce success; then in real life, most probably I will succeed. But even if I don't succeed, I shall keep rationally accepting myself and repeat that process until I do succeed.

The following YUPI items may interface with my REI's on CSP #2: CSB's #2, 13, 29, 33, and 35.

CSP #3:   I won't be able to accept myself until I get more self-confidence.

HELPFUL FACTS AND INSIGHTS

True believers in CSP #3 have the same problem as true believers in CSP #2 *plus* intense self-hate. But they confuse themselves by calling their self-hate "inability to accept themselves as failures."

Their logical but irrational goal is to make themselves so emotionally miserable that in self-defense they will give up their irrational high-failure self-confidence, which they mislabel "no self-confidence" or "not having enough self-confidence." All they achieve, though, is continued, useless self-hate. Now let's see why.

To refuse to accept themselves, people would have to reject themselves. To reject themselves, people would either have to send themselves away from themselves, or refuse to deal with themselves. Obviously, it's not possible for anyone to do either of those things.

Everywhere people go, they have to be there. Those facts persist even when people go insane and believe they are someone else. They are still their insane selves, incorrectly believing that they are someone else.

MY PRESCRIBED REI SCRIPT FOR CSB #3

I shall now mentally picture myself in a situation where I normally think CSP #3, but now I shall sincerely think: I shall always rationally give myself unconditional positive self-acceptance. I shall also calmly make sure that all of my efforts to do things are genuinely rational efforts. Then I shall rationally accept myself and the results of my efforts.

The following YUPI items may interfere with my REI's on CSP #3: CSB's #2, 13, 29, 31, and 35.

CSP #4: I am not as good a person as I can and should be.

HELPFUL FACTS AND INSIGHTS

True believers in CSP #4 usually have the self-defeating belief or attitude that their behavior defines them as human beings. When they have undesirable behaviors, they believe that proves they are undesirable people. In reality, all it proves is that they are FHB's (fallible human beings).

Fallible means having an incurable tendency to make mistakes. No matter how diligently people work to decrease their undesirable behaviors, their status as only FHB's never changes.

MY PRESCRIBED REI SCRIPT FOR CSP #4

I shall now mentally picture myself in a situation where I normally think CSP #4, but now I shall sincerely think: There are no good or bad people. There are only FHB's who behave in both desirable or good and undesirable or bad ways. Since I have no other choice than to be an FHB, it's absurd to believe that I ought to be something else. That's why I refuse to believe or try to act on that absurd idea anymore. Instead I shall diligently work to improve my undesirable behaviors while always giving myself unconditional positive self-acceptance.

The following NII's may interfere with my REI's on CSP #4: NII's #1 and 3.

CSP #5:   My life is worthless and unproductive.

HELPFUL FACTS AND INSIGHTS

True believers in CSP #5 usually dislike themselves intensely for both real and imagined reasons. They mislabel their self-dislike as "feeling that my life is worthless and unproductive." Then they use their incorrectly labeled self-dislike in these two irrational ways: (1) as proof that their lives are worthless and unproductive, and (2) to punish themselves for having presumably worthless, unproductive lives. Their irrational gut logic is: "I wouldn't *feel* worthless and unproductive if I weren't really that way."

Their self-dislike drains away their creative energy, so they stay undermotivated for productive activity, thereby completing their irrational psychoemotional circle.

MY PRESCRIBED REI SCRIPT FOR CSP #5

I shall now mentally picture myself in a situation where I normally think CSP #5, but now I shall sincerely think: There is no objectively valid way to judge people's lives as being worthwhile or worthless. That's why my life is as worthwhile for me as it now should be, even though it's not what I wanted to see. But until I can change it to what I want it to be, I shall give myself the unconditional positive self-acceptance that sane, intelligent, better coping people give themselves continually and automatically.

The following NII's may interfere with my REI's on CSP #5: NII's #4 and 3.

CSP #6: (Circle the ones that apply to you.) I'm too tall, too short, too dark-skinned, too light-skinned, too skinny, too fat, not masculine enough, not feminine enough, not intelligent enough. (List any other negative self-perceptions that you make.)

HELPFUL FACTS AND INSIGHTS

True believers in CSP #6 usually have the same problem believers in CSP's #4 and 5 have. Focus your self-help efforts on those YUPI items and you will get rid of your problems with CSP #6.

CSP #7: I am a phony.

HELPFUL FACTS AND INSIGHTS

True believers in CSP #7 dislike themselves intensely for their objective and imagined behavioral shortcomings. Here's what they usually mean when they say "I am a phony": They don't feel their most familiar emotions when they "act out" new ideas or new behaviors. Therefore, what they call "being a phony" is just natural, normal, and unavoidable cognitive-emotive dissonance. When these people understand that, they ignore their irrational fear of being a phony and practice until their new behaviors become habitual. Then CSP #7 quickly disappears.

Here's another common way true believers in CSP #7 make themselves miserable. They believe that if other people "really" get to know them, those people will dislike them. So these true believers usually become quite skilled at "people-pleasing" behaviors. Their people-pleasing behaviors usually produce the acceptance and approval by others that these people refuse to give to themselves.

Periodically, though, these true believers get intensely angry at themselves about their people-pleasing behaviors. Then they flip-flop from their popular people-pleasing behaviors into obnoxious behaviors. Their excuse is: "I'm just *sooo* sick of being a people-pleasing phony. I've decided to be my real self for a change."

Better coping people enjoy having the same people-pleasing behaviors that true believers in CSP #7 hate themselves for having.* These true believers incorrectly believe their people-pleasing behaviors prove that they are hopelessly dislikeable people.

With equally irrational fervor, these true believers hope to discover either that their assumed dislikableness has been their mistaken idea or that it's no longer a fact. That's another reason these true believers hate their people-pleasing behaviors. In their confused minds, if other people were to love them without their people-pleasing behaviors, that would prove that it really was a mistake to have believed that they were ever dislikable. So their flip-flops into obnoxious behaviors are those true believers' ways of seeing if people will like them without their people-pleasing behaviors. However, here's what always happens.

---

*These irrational romantics pine for the mythical, unconditional, romantic love; but sane, intelligent people are only willing to continually love people on the condition that they behave in lovable or otherwise people-pleasing ways.

The other people immediately withdraw their approval from these true believers. Then the true believers react with an intense fear of being left alone, without any friends at all. So they ultimately do another behavioral flip-flop back to their hated, but highly effective, people-pleasing behaviors.

In summary then, true believers in CSP #7 keep themselves in a painful three-way emotional bind: (1) They have an inaccurate, but sincere, negative self-perception; (2) They irrationally believe that both fate and other people are unfair to them; (3) They have normal, healthy desires for pleasant social acceptance and approval; but they refuse to give themselves healthy self-acceptance and approval.

MY PRESCRIBED REI SCRIPT FOR CSP #7

I shall now mentally picture myself in a situation where I normally think CSP #7, but now I shall sincerely think: There are many phony human beings. But they are all mannequins, most often seen in store windows. I am alive. Therefore, I can't ever be either a mannequin or a phony human being. Even when I die, I shall be my real dead self. So I am always my real self, both when I behave in my people-pleasing *and* in my obnoxious ways. But I'm good at people-pleasing behaviors, and they get me what I want; that's why I'm now making those behaviors my new personality traits.

The following YUPI items may interfere with my REI's on CSP #7: CSB's #5, 6, 10, 14, 16, and 17.

CSP #8: People use me and it upsets me.

HELPFUL FACTS AND INSIGHTS

True believers in CSP #8 either don't know, or they ignore, that "It" never does anything to anyone emotionally. People always do every emotional thing to themselves about "It." In addition, true believers in CSP #8 usually have a problem with self-dislike and/or self-defeating suspiciousness of other people's motivations.

When true believers in CSP #8 angrily say that they have been used, they do *not* mean they have been robbed or swindled. They mean that they believe their associates have gotten more benefits from associating with them than they (i.e., the true believers) have gotten; or they believe their associates have gotten different benefits from the association than they were "supposed to get."

These true believers either don't know or they ignore these facts: (1) No one can control the benefits other people get from associating with them; (2) Often people don't even know what benefits they want and/or are getting from associating with other people; (3) The only rational concern people can have about associating with others is whether or not they are getting for themselves enough personal benefits to justify continuing the association. If they aren't then it's rational to end it; but if they are, then it's rational to enjoy it.

MY PRESCRIBED REI SCRIPT FOR CSP #8

I shall now mentally picture myself in a situation where I normally think CSP #8, but now I shall sincerely think: Only by becoming a social hermit can I prevent people from doing what I call "using me;" that is, benefiting from associating with me. I therefore shall forget about being used and concentrate on enjoying my associations.

The "It-Monster" never does anything to me emotionally. I always do every emotional thing to myself about "It." I alone make myself angry and depressed when I believe someone has used me. But if no one has tricked me into doing the things I do or have done for them, I will *not* have been used; it will be irrational, therefore, to claim that I have been used, so I won't do that anymore.

The following YUPI items may interfere with my REI's on CSP #8: CSB's #6, 15, 21, 29, 30, 34, and 35.

CSP #9: It makes me angry at myself when I don't live up to my proven potential.

HELPFUL FACTS AND INSIGHTS

True believers in CSP #9 believe that proven past potential for certain performances is a guarantee for similar future performances. But that's a mistaken idea. Suppose, for example, that you earned all A's in school last year, but you now are earning all C's. Those facts would prove only that you had the proven potential to earn all A's last year, and you have the proven potential to earn all C's now. Granted, with greater effort, you may be able to earn all A's later, but you won't know that for sure until you actually make that greater effort and earn those A's.

People's current performances are always the only proof of their potential now. Also, that's the only performance people get paid for; so it's only their proven potential now that really counts.

Fortunately, it's very easy for people to improve their proven potential. They only have to improve their *next* performance; then they will have instantly improved their proven potential; and they will have lived up to it, too.

MY PRESCRIBED REI SCRIPT FOR CSP #9

I shall now mentally picture myself in a situation where I normally think CSP #9, but now I shall sincerely think: I always live up to my potential for my present performance. And that's the only proven potential that deserves my serious thought. Therefore, I shall look to my past performances only to get help in improving my current performances. Then both my performances *and* my proven potential will improve. In addition, I shall always remember that the "It-Monster" (the outside world) *never* does anything to me emotionally. Instead, I *always* do every emotional thing to myself about the various "It's" in my life. But I alone control which "It's" I react to and how much I react to them.

The following NII and YUPI items may interfere with my REI on CSP #9: NII #1, plus CSB's #1, 4, 8, 18, and 20.

CSP #10: It makes me feel just awful when people treat me unfairly or unjustly.

HELPFUL FACTS AND INSIGHTS

True believers in CSP #10 either don't know or they ignore that the "It-Monster" (their situation) never does anything to them emotionally. They always do every emotional thing to themselves about "It." Also, these people often have the habit of replacing the objective facts (described next) about what's fair and just with their arbitrary opinions about fairness and justices.

WHAT'S REALLY FAIR AND JUST

What's fair and just is whatever people agree is fair and just; or what's fair and just is whatever the people with recognized authority say fairness or justice is. The most common examples of such people are: parents, judges, bosses, elected or appointed officials, etc.

Unfortunately, most unhappy people believe that what's fair or just is what they want; and what's unfair or unjust is what they *don't* want. Those definitions work well only when you are dealing with yourself alone. But when you are dealing with someone else, the two of you first have to define what shall be fair or just, otherwise, only the people with enforceable authority can rationally talk about fairness and justice. Ignoring these facts causes people to confuse and needlessly upset themselves.

When honest people agree about fairness and justice beforehand, their disagreements will come only from mistaken perceptions. The Camera Check of Perceptions (Chapter 6) easily and quickly resolves such disagreements. But when people don't have prior agreements about fairness and justice, or if one is or both of the people are dishonest, then they have nothing to discuss. It will then be best for their lawyers to resolve the disagreement, or for all parties to rationally forget the matter.

MY PRESCRIBED REI SCRIPT FOR CSP #10

I shall now mentally picture myself in a situation where I normally think CSP #10, but now I shall sincerely think: I know and rationally accept that what's fair or just is whatever we agreed is fair and just. Or, fair or just is what the people who have enforceable authority about the issue say is fair or just. If neither of those conditions apply here, I shall forget about fairness and justice and deal as rationally as I can with the objective issues at hand.

The following YUPI items may interfere with my REI's on CSP #10: CSB's #29, 30, 33, 34, and 35.

CSP #11: It upsets me very much when things that really matter to me don't go right.

HELPFUL FACTS AND INSIGHTS

True believers in CSP #11 either don't know or they ignore that the "It-Monsters" (the fact and events in life) never do anything to anyone emotionally. People *always* do every emotional thing to themselves about "It." That's why where your emotional control is concerned, *you* are *It*. The useless distress caused by not knowing that fact often causes these true believers to develop emotional and/or psychosomatic problems.

Your mother (and other parent substitute) really was correct when she told you: "Dear, you don't have to get undesirably upset just because you don't get what you want. And remember, if at first you don't succeed, try more *rationally* the next time." That advice is still good today for absolutely anything.

MY PRESCRIBED REI SCRIPT FOR CSB #11

I shall now mentally picture myself in a situation where I normally think CSP #11, but now I shall sincerely think: Things always go right for the objective situation that exists at that moment. However, what's right for me at any specific moment may not be what I wanted; and, when it isn't; it's best for my emotional health and my coping ability to calmly accept and rationally deal with that fact. That means doing what I can to get what I want without having useless negative emotions.

The following CSB's may interfere with my REI's on CSP #11: CSB's #16, 17, 21, 24, 26, 28, 34, and 35.

CSP #12: No one cares enough about me emotionally.

HELPFUL FACTS AND INSIGHTS

CSP #12 is an excellent example of the intelligent-sounding noises people naively mistake for insight into their unhappiness. CSP #12 is only an emotionally confusing illusion, usually supported by one or more of the CSB's listed at the end of this discussion.

The only people who know if enough emotional caring is being done are the people who are doing it. Your only rational concern is whether or not your associates are treating you well enough for you to *rationally* continue your relationship with them. If they are, enjoy it; if they are not, rationally try to influence them to treat you better; but if you fail, rationally end that relationship and start another one with someone else.

Granted, if you are a dependent child, ending the relationship may not yet be possible, but remember: Childhood is only a temporary disadvantage. *And no one* can avoid it but every sane, intelligent child (or adult) can learn to deal rationally with their involuntarily dependent states.

MY PRESCRIBED REI SCRIPT FOR CSP #12

I shall now mentally picture myself in a situation where I normally think CSP #12, but now I shall sincerely think: Caring is an emotional state. The only people who can know if caring is occurring are the people who create that state. And, however much or little caring people do, that's exactly enough for them at that moment. Those are the most important facts about caring you can always be sure about. But it would be silly to expect anyone else to care more, or even as much about me as I do. I shall make sure, therefore, to care enough about myself to refuse to be irrationally concerned about how much others care about me.

The following YUPI items may interfere with my REI's on CSP #12: CSB's #6, 11, 15, 16, 17, 25, 29, 30, 32, 34, and 35.

CSP #13: The solution to my emotional problems is for certain people to care enough about me to fulfill my emotional dependency needs.

HELPFUL FACTS AND INSIGHTS

This is a popular variation of the intelligent-sounding noise true believers in CSP #12 naively mistake for useful insight into why they are unhappy. Like CSP #12, however, CSP #13 is merely an emotionally confusing illusion, supported by one or more of the CSB's listed for CSP #12.

The word *need* means that you can not live or get along without something. But you *are* alive and getting along. Therefore, what you are calling "your emotional dependency needs" can not be objective needs; they are only personal desires or irrational demands. If they were rational demands, you would succeed in getting them met on your own terms.

MY PRESCRIBED REI SCRIPT FOR CSP #13

I shall now mentally picture myself in a situation where I normally think CSP #13, but now I shall sincerely think: There are no emotional dependency needs that mature, healthy people cannot fulfill for themselves. In fact, people themselves are the *only* ones who can fill their emotional dependency needs. By rationally accepting these two facts, I instantly free myself to have naturally happy relationships with anyone I can, instead of making myself act as if I were an emotional parasite on other people.

The following CSB's may interefere with my REI's on CSP # 13: CSB's #6, 16, 17, 29, and 34.

CSP #14: I have tried to change myself but I just can't do it.

HELPFUL FACTS AND INSIGHTS

Trying without succeeding is the proven formula for failures; *doing* what is necessary to succeed is the *only* proven formula for success.

Usually, true believers in CSP #14 just try to do what's necessary to change themselves; or, they merely proclaim that they *should have* already achieved their desired new behavioral goals, even though they have done nothing, or very little to achieve them.

To impress upon yourself the futility of merely trying to do something, try this: Sit ten feet away from a closed door; then stretch out your arm and try to open the door without moving; then get up and do what's necessary to open it. Afterward, objectively point out to yourself the important difference between merely trying to do something and actually doing what's necessary to accomplish it.

MY PRESCRIBED REI SCRIPT FOR CSP #14

I shall now mentally picture myself in a situation where I normally think CSP #14, but now I shall sincerely think: I have not suffered any known brain damage since I learned my present, undesirable behaviors. That's why I can be reasonably certain that I still have at least as much brain power available to erase and replace my undesirable behaviors as I had when I learned them. That's all the brain power I need to achieve my better coping and natural happiness goals.

The following YUPI items may interfere with my REI's on CSP #14: CSB's #1, 3, 4, 5, 6, 7, 8, 18, 21, 22, 26, 27, and 28.

CSP #15: I am just unlucky.

MY PRESCRIBED REI SCRIPT FOR CSP #15

I shall now mentally picture myself in a situation where I normally think CSP #15, but now I shall sincerely think: Luck is nothing more than the most logical consequence of people's rational or irrational habitual approaches to life. So-called unlucky people pursue life in irrationally prepared ways. Consequently, when fortuitous situations arise, true believers in CSP #15 only rarely are able to take advantage of them. On the other hand, so-called lucky people consistently pursue life in rationally prepared ways. When fortuitous situations arise, therefore, these people are ideally prepared to take advantage of them; and they actually take advantage of them. Only the behaviorally naive call that "being lucky." Therefore, I shall forget about luck and keep myself rationally prepared to take advantage of the opportunities that I rationally hope to get by being prepared.

The following YUPI items may interfere with my REI's on CSP #15, CSB's #5, 7, 17, 22, 25, 26, 28, and 36.

CSP #16:   I have to stay somewhat tense until I do the important thing that I have to do; otherwise, I forget to do them.

HELPFUL FACTS AND INSIGHTS

True believers in CSP #16 usually have problems with self-defeating procrastination. That's because these true believers excessively motivate themselves with self-threat motivation. Therefore, in addition to excessive task-related anxiety, these people have all the other problems excessive self-threat motivation causes. To fully appreciate the sinister nature of this widely popular means of self-motivation, let's take a brief yet in-depth look at it.

SELF-THREAT MOTIVATION

Most people perceive three main groups of personel tasks in everyday life: (1) the "I-want-to-do" tasks, (2) the "I-don't-want-to-do" tasks, and (3) the "I-don't-want-to,-but-I-have-to-do" tasks. Usually normal, intelligent children quickly learn the next fact extremely well: Failure to perform the "I-don't-want-to,-but-I-have-to" tasks results either in the threat of dreaded punishment or the dreaded punishment itself.

In the minds of impressionable young children, both threats of and the actual punishments quickly become "terrible" or "awful" events, to be avoided at all cost. Understandably, then, sincerely thinking the idea "I-have-to" quickly becomes the most reliable way young children have of generating the fear they need to motivate themselves to do their important "I-don't-want-to" tasks. That way of motivating themselves works so well for most children that as adults they continue to use it almost exclusively for their important "I-don't-want-to-do" tasks.

When most people get a disliked task that's in their best interest, therefore, they immediately think: I have to do it. If they instantly feel strong self-motivational fear, they do the task immediately. But that's rare, except when people are speeding down the highway and suddenly see flashing red and blue lights. Usually most people think: I have to do it. Then they immediately put off getting started. But they start repeatedly reminding themselves that they still have to do that disliked task, and they start feeling mildly, but progressively, anxious. After repeating: "I have to do it" enough times, they feel so uncomfortably anxious about their inaction that they start doing the task and complete it ASAP. That's how they turn off their self-induced, motivating fear until they get another "I-don't-want-to,-but-I-have-to" task.

The only good thing about self-threat motivation is it usually gets the job done. Everything else about it is bad and ultimately makes this method of self-motivation ineffective. That's because sincerely thinking I-have-to is the same as believing "I have no choice, or I'm forced to do it." Chapter 10 gives you a detailed discussion of why such beliefs cause severe problems in self-motivation. To cope best with CSP #16, therefore, I refer you to that discussion and its prescribed REI script.

CSP #17: When I hurt other people emotionally, that fact hurts me more than it hurts them.

HELPFUL FACTS AND INSIGHTS

True believers in CSP #17 have not yet learned that people never do anything to other people emotionally. Instead, people always do every emotional thing to themselves with their beliefs and attitudes about people and events.

Yes, these true believers can and may help others hurt themselves; that's easy; just do what those others believe you shouldn't do. But the hurting will still be the hurting people's own doing. Fortunately though, by learning their emotional A,B,C's and the

Five Rational Questions (see Chapter 1), people can just as easily make their interactions with other people mutually helpful.

MY PRESCRIBED REI SCRIPT FOR CSP #17

I shall now mentally picture myself in a situation where I normally think CSP #17, but now I shall sincerely think: The "It-Monster" (the outside world) *never does anything to me* (or anyone else) *emotionally*. I (like everyone else) *always do every emotional thing to myself about "IT."* I shall make a continuous rational effort to avoid helping others hurt themselves. But even if I fail, I shall refuse to give myself any more emotional pain about my failure than actually helps me cope best with that event.

The following CSB's may interfere with my REI's on CSP #17: CSB's #10, 11, 17, 21, 22, 25, 27, and 34.

CSP #18: If someone does me wrong, I feel that I just have to get even.

HELPFUL FACTS AND INSIGHTS

· True believers in CSP #18 usually are habitual gut-thinking injustice collectors. They go through life with a mental and sometimes a real tally book of the injustices (mostly imaginary) for which they believe that have to retaliate. Their retaliations, however, most often trigger secondary retaliations from the targeted other people. So in addition to their time-consuming tally bookkeeping, true believers in CSP #18 spend lots of time planning self-defenses against the retaliations that they have provoked.

To get even for a wrong, people must commit a second wrong to match the first one; but that second wrong never corrects the first one; it either matches or exceeds it, plus creates a logical reason for a third retaliatory wrong, persistent anger, and a never-ending series of retaliatory wrongs. Rather than trying to get even, therefore, it's best for people to use the Five Rules for Rational Thinking to help themselves discover emotionally healthy ways to handle their interactions with people who they believe have done them wrong.

MY PRESCRIBED REI SCRIPT FOR CSP #18

I shall now mentally picture myself in a situation where I normally think CSP #18, but now I shall sincerely think: I do not feel that I have to get even; I only believe it. But it's an irrational belief, because to get even for an unjust act, I will have to treat the alleged guilty people unjustly. If I don't, then I will not have gotten even. But when I treat people unjustly, I give them a logical reason to treat me unjustly—to get even with me. That then gives me another logical reason to treat them unjustly, and on and on. That vicious circle could repeat itself forever. I rationally refuse to live or to die in that self-defeating way.

The following CSB's may interfere with my REI's on CSP #18: CSB's #6, 20, 24, and 32.

CSP #19:   I don't let little things bother me; but if someone keeps piling stuff on me that no one should stand for, I really blow my lid.

HELPFUL FACTS AND INSIGHTS

True believers in CSP #19 usually are habitual injustice collectors also. They, too, keep a mental tally book of real and imagined injustices. These people often appear to be fun-loving and easygoing, but they secretly are tallying up their "injustices." Consequently, they maintain varying levels of chronic hostility, which they suddenly release when they fill up a tally sheet.

If you have not already done so, thoroughly read CSP #18 and do one or two days of REI using its REI script. Then do three days of REI using the REI script for CSP #19.

MY PRESCRIBED REI SCRIPT FOR CSP #19

I shall now mentally picture myself in a situation where I normally think CSP #19, but now I shall sincerely think: Physical things are the only things people can pile upon another person. No one is doing that to me; so I shall stop accusing people of doing it to me. What I meant was that I tally up real and imaginary injustices and mentally relive them until I can justify having a temper tantrum, and then I have a temper tantrum. But, because I dislike that childish behavior, I am now mentally practicing having calm, rational discussions with people about my complaints.

The following CSB's may interfere with my REI's on CSP #19: CSB's #16, 17, 20, 21, 30, and 32.

CSP #20: When people really love each other, good old, "let-it-all-hang-out, but fair lover's fights" give them good feelings of closeness to each other.

HELPFUL FACTS AND INSIGHTS

Usually, true believers in CSP #20 are injustice-collecting mental-tally bookkeepers, too. In addition, they have an intense fear of rejection. Their incessant injustice collecting keeps them feeling some degree of hostility toward most people they know well, and especially toward their romantic partners. When the intensity of their hostility surpasses that of their fear of rejection, they "pick" one of their so-called good old, let-it-all-hang-out, but fair lover's fights.

After their "fair lover's fights," these true believers have a strong tendency to feel painfully anxious. They are afraid that this time their loved ones just might have gotten angry enough to terminate their relationship. To prevent or to relieve their developing panic about that possibility, these true believers immediately start behaving in an extremely loving way toward their now angry loved ones.

The more resistant their loved ones react, the more romantically ardent these true believers become. Daily, they make ostentatious displays of seemingly unswerving romantic love for their mates. These impassioned campaigns are equalled in passion only by the viciousness these people often show during their so-called fair lover's fights.

Their powerfully persuasive behavior may continue for days—sometimes even weeks or months; then it ends abruptly in one of three ways: (1) It can end in a passion-filled, mutually forgiving lovemaking event. In relatively new relationships, this is the most common ending. (2) In older relationships, these "after-fight" impassioned campaigns often end in another vicious, but "fair lover's fight" with the hostile breakup of the relationship. (3) The "after-fight" impassioned campaign often ends in a coldly logical announcement by the true believer in CSP #20 that it's best for both of them to break off their relationship and get on with their lives. "It's just not worth it."

The "It" they refer to is their own increasingly painful fear of being left alone that has been motivating their most recent loving behaviors. Until these true believers decide to break off their relationships, they self-deceptively mislabel their painful fear of being left alone as intense romantic love. That self-deception often leads to statements like "I love him or her so much it hurts; it really and truly hurts." But after their impassioned "lovemaking makeups," these true believers make insightful-sounding noises like: "It must be love because even the hurting feels so good."

THE MAIN INSIGHTS TO REMEMBER

The "good feelings of closeness" true believers in CSP #20 describe is largely the pleasant relief caused by the rapid decrease in their self-created painful fear of romantic rejection. Psychoemotionally, therefore, these people put themselves in a situation that's like people who sit on nails so that they can feel *sooooo* good when they jump up.

That routine works, but I don't recommend it as a way to feel good. Instead, I recommend that people avoid or eliminate both the "nails in their romantic chairs" plus their belief in the so-called fair lover's fights.

Except in amateur or professional boxing and wrestling, fighting normally is motivated by anger and *never* love. Anger is an urge to harm or destroy. Love is an urge to protect and keep. So the concept of "fair lover's fights" is as sensible as the concept of humanely killing in war. War means killing—without the killing, there is no war. No matter how nicely people describe humane killings, the corpses are just as dead.

MY PRESCRIBED REI SCRIPT FOR CSP #20

I shall now mentally picture myself in a situation where I normally think CSP #20, but now I shall sincerely think: My so-called fair-lover's fights are no less painful than "unfair lover's fights." No matter how sincerely I believe that my intense anger and fear-motivated, after-fight lovemaking leads to genuine, loving feelings of closeness, my stimuli for those fights are still urges to harm, if not destroy. That just "ain't love," nor does it lead to lasting, loving closeness. That's why I shall stop that nonsense today. I shall rationally deal with my complaints long before I feel inclined to harm my romantic mate.

The following CSB's may interfere with my REI's on CSP #20: CSB's #20 through 32.

CSP #21: The very time I decide to be carefree and loose, something bad always happens.

HELPFUL FACTS AND INSIGHTS

Virtually everybody has that perception sometimes, but these true believers are magical worriers. They have the (usually unnoticed, but often clearly recognized and admitted) attitude that worrying somehow protects them from the events they fear. Understandably, therefore, they are afraid *not* to be afraid; so they diligently worry every day about their important concerns. Consequently, their normal daily emotional states usually vary between minimal anxiety and quiet semi-panic.

Why do these sane, intelligent people learn the irrational attitude that worrying helps them? Easily! They insist on doing gut thinking (see Chapter 8) instead of brain thinking. Or, as one of my patients said:

A RATIONAL LOOK AT GUT THINKING VERSUS BRAIN THINKING

As explained in Chapter 8, gut thinking means accepting and rejecting ideas or actions solely on the basis of how you feel in response to those ideas or actions. Gut thinkers have the incorrect belief that their emotional feelings give them more useful insight and information than their thoughts give them. In reality, though, gut thinking only tells you if you are then reacting to new ideas or to your old beliefs and attitudes.

Gut thinkers either don't know that fact, or they ignore it. That's why they maintain a blinding focus on their incorrect belief that what they say they feel accurately reflects what is objectively is happening, or that it predicts what is going to happen. Here's how people learn that superstition.

Imagine that last week you felt anxious during your math test, and you flunked it. Your gut thinking would be: I just knew that I was going to flunk it; I felt it. Then imagine that today you feel anxious about your scheduled English test. Your gut thinking would probably be: I feel that I'm going to flunk this English test. Then if you do flunk it (and if you are like most gut thinkers), you probably will jump to this incorrect conclusion: I knew that I was going to flunk it; I felt it all along. Now let's see why that conclusion would be an incorrect interpretation of these experiences.

The A,B,C's of human emotions clearly demonstrate this fact: People feel anxious *only* because they believe something bad is going to happen. Without that underlying belief, they could not feel anxious.

For the exam examples to apply to you, you would have had these two beliefs (1) "I probably don't know enough to pass this math test" and (2) "It will be awful if I flunk it." Those two beliefs would have made you feel anxious about the real possibility of flunking that test. What would your pre–English exam anxiety have proven? Only that you had the same beliefs about the English exam that you had about your math exam.

But what if you had *incorrectly* believed that you knew enough to safely pass that math test? Then you would have felt calm, if not happy, during the test; still you would have flunked it. On the other hand, (as is usually the case with intelligent magical worriers) what if you had felt anxious about flunking the test but had passed it? Afterward would you have said "I felt that I was going to pass it?" Not if you are a typical gut thinker. A typcal gut thinker would still say: "I felt that I was going to flunk; but *luckily* I was mistaken." But would that have been the reality? Or course not.

You would have mislabeled your preexam anxiety—"feeling that I'm going to flunk." But (if you are a typical gut thinker) you either wouldn't have known, or you would have ignored these three facts: (1) You felt anxious only because you believed it's bad to flunk tests. (2) You sincerely thought that you might not know enough to pass that test. (3) Being a magical worrier, you were afraid not to be afraid of flunking that test.

Brain thinking means accepting or rejecting ideas or actions solely on the basis of how much objective evidence supports the idea or action. That's why brain thinking tells you if your present belief, emotions, and physical actions are appropriate for your current situation. In the English test example, your brain thinking would have been: I'm feeling anxious because I believe it would be bad for me to flunk this test. But feeling anxious about possibly flunking is helpful only if I can then study some more. Obviously, I can't study anymore now. So feeling anxious now can't help me; but it might well interfere with me doing as well as I can. Also, I believe that I know more than enough to easily pass this test. But if I'm wrong, then I'm going to flunk. That's an unavoidable fact. However, whether I flunk or pass, I will feel better if I calmly, instead of anxiously, take the test. So I'll focus on calmly answering all the questions to the best of my ability.

Mother Nature seems to have intended for sane, intelligent people to do brain thinking instead of gut thinking, especially when they try to decide how best to cope with important life events. Yes, gut thinkers almost always are sane, intelligent people, too. That's why, in addition to their gut thinking, they usually do enough brain thinking to be successful, often highly successful. But here's their problem. Gut thinkers are usually more sensitive than most people are to their beliefs and attitudes. So while gut thinkers await the outcome of personally important events, they feel more intensely anxious than most people feel about the real but remote possibilities of dreaded results.

Unfortunately, these people believe that any anxious feeling is a "feeling that something bad is going to happen." And what these true believers call being "carefree and loose" is being just a little bit less worried than usual about remotely possible, personally dreaded events happening.

Why did I say "remotely possible . . . dreaded events"? Because with each of their important events, true believers in CSP #21 worry about a dreaded result occurring, yet *only rarely* do these dreaded events occur. In these people's minds, therefore, their successes, especially their important successes, are almost always mentally associated with their intense worry about failure. These true believers misinterpret that fact and jump to the erroneous conclusions that (1) worrying prevents their dreaded events from happening, and (2) failure to worry will let if not cause their dreaded events to happen.

The latter incorrect conclusion is usually based on this rare chain of events. Because no one is perfect, all magical worriers have occasionally slipped up and been only mildly worried about a dreaded event that actually happened. Remember, though, normally these people worry and their dreaded events don't happen. Predictably, therefore, they now incorrectly conclude: "Ah, ha!! I knew all along that it was going to happen. I felt it and if I had just paid more attention to my feelings [meaning—if I had just worried more about that dreaded result], it just might not have happened."

MY PRESCRIBED REI SCRIPT FOR CSP #21

I shall now mentally picture myself in a situation where I normally think CSP #21, but now I shall sincerely think: My magical worry is really being afraid not to be afraid. But my magical worry makes me *more* anxious than I need to be to get myself to do all that I am willing or able to do to protect myself from my dreaded events. Worry is also the one energy-draining thing I or anyone can always do. That's why when I worry, I create the illusion that I am actually working effectively to protect myself. But I now see clearly that worry does *not* protect me from anything. All my worry does is make me needlessly miserable. That's why I now use the ISRM (Instant Stress-Reducing Maneuver) to keep myself from worrying any more about anything. Yes, I shall continue to be rationally concerned about my dreaded events, but *never* worried about them.

The following CSB's may interfere with my REI's on CSP #21: CSB's #19 and 36.

CSP #22: It's wrong to believe that I am the most important person in the world to me.

HELPFUL FACTS AND INSIGHTS

True believers in CSP #22 believe that certain other people are more important to them than they are to themselves. Their sincere but incorrect belief blinds them to this fact: It's impossible for any other person to be more important to a person than that person is to him or herself. The next example demonstrates that fact.

Imagine this event: You are in a life-threatening situation with someone whom you believe is more important to you than you are. Only one of you can survive. Your belief in the greater importance of that other person would oblige you to volunteer to die so that he or she could live. Otherwise, your more important person would die and you, a less important person, would live. That event would invalidate your belief that the other person is more important to you than you are.

So let's assume that you choose to die so that your more important person can live. *What would your death really prove?* Only that *you* really *were* more important to you than anyone else. Why? Because you would have been the only person who could have done for you what you wanted done—namely, ensure the survival of your more highly valued person. So even your sacrificial death would prove that you are the most important person in the world to you.

A COMMON QUESTION

Won't acting on the idea that I'm the most important person in the world to me make me selfishly violate the rights of other people? No, no, no. Just the opposite will be the case; assuming, of course, that you think rationally.

Rationally thinking people know that each person is the most important person in the world to him or herself. That knowledge leads rationally thinking people to protect, rather than violate, other people's rights. Why? Because they know that such action is the only key to healthy group living. And rationally thinking people almost *always* prefer healthy group living to being a hermit. Understandably, then, rationally thinking people tend to be the most humanistic people.

MY PRESCRIBED REI SCRIPT FOR CSP #22

I shall now mentally picture myself in a situation where I normally think CSP #22, but now I shall sincerely think: Both in my life and death, I am always the most important person in the world to me. It's best for my mental, emotional, and physical health, therefore, for me to always remember and rationally act on that fact. The best way to do that is to always put my needs in front of everyone else's; what is good for me has to be ultimately good for everyone who depends on me.

The following CSB's may interfere with my REI's on CSP #22: CSB's #1, 3, 4, 14, 16, 17, 29, and 34.

CSP #23:   I can't concentrate the way I should.

HELPFUL FACTS AND INSIGHTS

There could be a medical problem that's interfering with your ability to concentrate. By all means, therefore, check out that possibility with your physician. If you are physically healthy, then most likely you are just a victim of CSP #23.

True believers in CSP #23 either don't know about or they ignore the concept of rational should's in favor of the concept of magical irrational should's. Before taking the prescription for CSP #23, I suggest that you carefully review NII #1 in Chapter 10.

MY PRESCRIBED REI SCRIPT FOR CSP #23

I shall now mentally picture myself in a situation where I normally think CSP #23, but now I shall sincerely think: *Everything is always exactly as it now should be, even though it's not what I wanted for me.* Therefore, whatever way I now concentrate is exactly the way I should now be concentrating. That's why I refuse to upset myself about it anymore. But I shall calmly do what I can to make my concentration more like I want it to be.

CSP #24:   The very time I decide to trust people, they always let me down.

HELPFUL FACTS AND INSIGHTS

True believers in CSP #24 usually have a strong self-defeating desire to control other people. These true believers also tend to make inappropriate demands on other people, which those other people often reject or ignore. In response to that, these true believers make themselves angry or depressed. Then they compound their confusion by believing that their self-induced anger or depression proves those other people really did let them down.

MY PRESCRIBED REI SCRIPT FOR CSP #24

I shall now mentally picture myself in a situation where I normally think CSP #24, but now I shall sincerely think: If the people I trust consistently prove to be untrustworthy, I need to improve my method for deciding whom to trust. For example, it would be best for me to judge people less on the basis of how I feel about them (gut thinking) and more on the basis of my rational thinking about them. I know that all personal behavioral improvements start with improved thinking. So, I shall use the Five Rational Questions to improve my thinking about who to trust.

The following CSB's may interfere with my REI's on CSP #24: CSB's #16, 17, 24, 32, and 35.

CSP #25: The world is cold, cruel, and unfeeling.

HELPFUL FACTS AND INSIGHTS

CSP #25 usually interlocks with CSP #24. So if you have not already done REI using the REI script for CSP #24, follow this routine: Thoroughly study CSP #24 and alternate daily REI's for four days using the REI scripts of CSP #24 and #25. Then go to your next highly scored YUPI item.

MY PRESCRIBED REI SCRIPT FOR CSP #25

I shall now mentally picture myself in a situation where I normally think CSP #25, but now I shall sincerely think: The words *cruel* and *unfeeling* are fine for describing people's behaviors, but those words are inappropriate for describing the world. Granted, the weather can be cold and warm, but the world is never cruel and unfeeling, nor is the world ever kind and feeling. The world just is as it is. It's only people's beliefs about the world that make it appear to be as each person experiences it. That's why I can easily improve my experiences of the world by erasing and replacing my beliefs about it. That's what I shall do immediately now that I have used the Five Rational Questions to show me the irrational ideas I need to erase and replace.

The following CSB's may interfere with my REI's on CSP #25: CSB's #5, 11, 15, 17, 29, 30, 33, and 34.

CSP #26:   Only really stupid people get used or taken advantage of.

HELPFUL FACTS AND INSIGHTS

True believers in CSP #26 usually dislike and try to reject themselves; they believe that they are stupid, or at least strongly suspect that they are. They also believe that if their stupidity were revealed to significant other people, they, too, would dislike and reject them. Those two beliefs explain why these people are afraid of someone taking advantage of them and thereby revealing their imagined stupidity.

"Stupid," however, most accurately labels people who can't learn anything. Only rarely will such people be able to live outside of mental institutions. Also, the undesirable but *learned* behaviors of the people whom you call stupid proves that they were capable of learning those behaviors. Unless their brain power has been completely destroyed since then, they can still learn other behaviors; therefore, they can't be stupid.

True believers in CSP #26 ignore that fact as well as the next one. Stupid people (i.e., people who can't learn anything) don't have anything that's worth trying to get. That's why sane, intelligent people would not waste their time taking advantage of them. Only equally stupid people would ever try to take advantage of stupid people. Fortunately, there probably won't ever be any such real people in your life.

MY PRESCRIBED REI SCRIPT FOR CSP #26

I shall now mentally picture myself in a situation where I normally think CSP #26, but now I shall sincerely think: Even if stupid people do exist outside by imagination, I certainly am *not* one of them. So, I refuse to be afraid anymore that being taken advantage of will prove that I'm stupid. But in spite of my most rational thinking, someone may still take advantage of me. That won't be awful or terrible; though it may well be inconvenient. Still, all it will prove is that I'm a fallible human being who some other fallible human being took advantage of. I shall then deal with that situation as rationally as I can and rationally get on with my life.

The following CSB's may interfere with my REI's on CSP #26: CSB's #1, 15, 19, 24, and 25.

CSP #27: Some people are just plain worthless; or they are so otherwise despicable that they deserve to be hated, if not damned.

HELPFUL FACTS AND INSIGHTS

True believers in CSP #27 usually have a severe Jehovah complex. That means they have the strong but unnoticed attitude that what they will or want to occur should occur, no matter what. And, when (as is often the case) their wills or wants are not gratified, these people make themselves painfully angry, but they angrily accuse the "It-Monster" or other people of having made them angry. That irrational belief gives these true believers a logical but very irrational reason to hate and damn those other people.

MY PRESCRIBED REI SCRIPT FOR CSP #27

I shall now mentally picture myself in a situation where I normally think CSP #27, but now I shall sincerely think: All people are equal as fallible human beings. Therefore, as human beings, every person is as objectively worthless and worthwhile as the next person. It's best for my emotional health, therefore, to rationally accept everyone; in addition, it's best to deal with people's behaviors as rationally as I can and refuse to try to estimate their worth as human beings, or the hypothetical appropriateness of damning them. It's also best for me to replace my Jehovah complex with this reality: Everything is always exactly as it now should be, even though it's not what I wanted to see. But I'm not God; therefore, this event is as it now has to be. Still, I shall do what I am willing and able to make it the way I want it to be for me.

The following CSB's may interfere with my REI's on CSP #27: CSB's #6, 8, 20, 27, and 32.

CSP #28:   When people try to make rational sense out of their emotions, they lose their creativity and become nonfeeling robots.

HELPFUL FACTS AND INSIGHTS

True believers in CSP #28 often are emotionally miserable; in addition, they often are self-styled artists and musicians who excuse and romanticize their self-destructive emotional control with the irrational idea that their irrational emotions reveal their artistic creativity. It is a fact that many of these people are quite talented and creative, but because their emotional control is so irrational, they are much more emotionally miserable than equally talented but rationally creative people ever allow themselves to be.

MY PRESCRIBED REI SCRIPT FOR CSP #28

I shall now mentally picture myself in a situation where I normally think CSP #28, but now I shall sincerely think: My creativity and talent are my birthrights, given to me by Mother Nature. Therefore, I do not have to be emotionally miserable to deserve or to reveal them. My emotional misery is self-induced, triggered by my miserable beliefs and attitudes. It's best for my emotional health, therefore, to use the Five Questions of Rational Self-Counseling to improve my emotional control. Then, I and every other interested person will be able to enjoy my talent and creativity for the longest possible time.

The following CSB's may interfere with my REI's on CSP #28: CSB's #22, 23, and 27.

CHAPTER 16

Prescriptions for Coping Better with Common Sense Beliefs (CSB's)

Instantly Helpful Insights

The instructions for this chapter are the same as those for Chapter 15. Please read those instructions now, if you have not already read them. If you think any CSB is rational for you, use the Five Rational Questions (as shown in Chapter 12) to check it.

An Important Fact to Remember

You didn't learn your CSB's in three days; and you are not going to completely replace any one of them with the suggested REI script in just three days. But by doing daily REI's as directed, your powerful brain will still be working in your favor, even after you go on to new YUPI items. And, if you end each instance of your undesirable behavior with just *one to three minutes* of corrective REI, you will most quickly replace your undesirable behavior with your desired better coping skill.

The Common Sense Beliefs

CSB #1: I believe I ought to or should be different from the way I am. (This CSB covers all such statements as "I'm too skinny, I'm too fat, I'm not intelligent enough, tall enough, feminine or masculine enough, etc.)

HELPFUL FACTS AND INSIGHTS

True believers in CSB #1 usually have chronic self-dislike, anger, guilt and depression, which they mislabel as feelings of inferiority. But there are no inferior people. Therefore, there are no genuine feelings of inferiority. What people call feelings of inferiority is really a combination of self-anger and shame triggered by their irrational belief that they are inferior people. That insight frees people to accept themselves unconditionally and focus on erasing and replacing their self-anger and shame with better coping skill and natural happiness.

MY PRESCRIBED REI SCRIPT FOR CSB #1

I shall now mentally picture myself in a situation where I normally think CSB #1, but I shall sincerely think: For emotionally healthy self-control, I must remember that, just like everyone else, I am always exactly as I now should be even though it's different from what I wanted to see. That's why I shall rationally do the things I can and am willing to do to make my situation exactly the way I want it to be. But until then, I shall use the ISRM to keep myself as pleasantly calm naturally as I now think it's best for me to be.

The following CSP's may interfere with your REI's: CSP's #2, 6, 9, 14, 22, and 26.

CSB #2:   I believe that I would like and accept myself better if I had more self-confidence.

HELPFUL FACTS AND INSIGHTS

The REI scripts for this CSB are the same as those for CSP's #2, and 3 in Chapter 15. Alternate them in daily REI's for four consecutive days.

CSB #3:   I believe I ought to be or should be a better person than I am.

HELPFUL FACTS AND INSIGHTS

True believers in CSB #3 usually have problems with self-dislike and depression.

MY PRESCRIBED REI SCRIPT FOR CSB #3

I shall now mentally picture myself in a situation where I normally think CSB #3, but I shall think: There are no objectively better or worse people. There are only better or worse personal behaviors for certain situations. I shall therefore behave in this better way. (Actually picture yourself behaving in the better way you desire and have already chosen for that situation. Then imagine yourself actually having the logical thoughts and emotional feelings that are most logical for your new behavior.) Regardless of my objective success or failure, I shall always give myself unconditional, positive self-acceptance because I'm all I have and all I need to give myself a naturally happy life.

The following NII's and CSP's may interfere with my corrective REI's for CSB #3: NII #4 and CSP's #1, 3, 6, 14, and 22.

CSB: #4:   I believe all people should live lives that are generally considered to be worthwhile and productive.

HELPFUL FACTS AND INSIGHTS

People who score higher than 2 on CSB #4 often get depressed, because they believe they are worthless human beings. Next is my highly effective maneuver for helping people to give up quickly that self-defeating idea. I say: "Pick up the telephone and call a local undertaker, one whom you do not know personally. Then ask what the minimum price of your funeral would be. That answer will tell you that dead you are worth quite a bit to a total stranger who doesn't know you or care about you as a living person. It seems to me, therefore, that it's only sane and logical to believe that alive you could easily be worth at least that much to yourself. In any case, you will have proven that you are not completely worthless. By completely depressing yourself, therefore, about your *in*completely worthless self, you are being completely unfair to yourself. I don't believe that you would encourage depressed strangers to be that unfair to themselves, would you?"

I've never had a nonpsychotic person to answer, "Yes." That's why I then ask: "Well, why not be as kind to yourself as you would be to strangers?" The people who have been sincere about helping themselves then rapidly learn how to cope better. The others just make irrational excuses and miserably wait for a miracle to solve their problem.

MY PRESCRIBED REI SCRIPT FOR CSB #4

I shall now mentally picture myself in a situation where I normally think CSB #4, but I shall sincerely think: Just like everyone's life, my life is always as productive and worthwhile as it now should be, even though it's different from what I wanted to see. So until I make my life the way I want it to be, I shall keep myself as rationally calm naturally as I now think it's best for me to be. That's the only kind and fair thing for me to do to myself.

The following NII's and CSP's may interfere with my corrective REI's: NII's #2 and 4 and CSP's #4, 5, 6, 9, 14, and 22.

CSB #5: I believe that if I act differently from my usual self, I'll be a phony person and I hate phonies.

HELPFUL FACTS AND INSIGHTS

True believers in CSB #5 usually want self-improvement and they often read many self-help books. But they rarely make significant personal changes. That's because CSB #5 gives people the Irrational Gooney Bird Syndrome.

Irrational Gooney Birds fly backward. They believe that where they've been is more real, genuine, and important than where they are going. With reference to people, all habitual behaviors, even irrational behaviors, feel more real, genuine, and important than new, rational behaviors feel at first. Only after enough practice behaving rationally will new behaviors begin to feel as real, genuine, and important as the old behaviors feel. (See CSB's #5 and 21 in Chapters 12 and 13 for the prescribed REI's for this item.)

CSB #6: I believe that a person's behavior shows what type of human being that person is.

HELPFUL FACTS AND INSIGHTS

Honest scores higher than 2 on CSB #6 usually indicate neurotic perfectionism and the self-defeating fear of making mistakes. Understandably, these people resist new ideas and new ways of doing things. That fact often makes these people appear to be lazy, if not downright stupid. In reality, though, they usually are intelligent and willing workers when their fear of making mistakes is low enough.

MY PRESCRIBED REI SCRIPT FOR CSB #6

I shall now mentally picture myself in a situation where I normally think CSB #6, but I shall sincerely think: My behavior only describes my behavior—never me as a human being. Therefore, I shall rationally reject my undesirable behavior, but I shall always give myself unconditional positive self-acceptance at all times.

The following CSP's may interfere with my corrective REI's for CSB #6: CSP's #7, 8, 12, 13, 14, 18, and 25.

CSB #7: I believe that I am a born worrier.

HELPFUL FACTS AND INSIGHTS

People who score higher than 2 on CSB #7 usually have high levels of chronic anxiety, mainly because they are *afraid not to be afraid*. They believe their worry somehow protects them from the things they worry about. For a more detailed description of that irrational belief, see CSP's #16 and 21 in Chapter 12.

MY PRESCRIBED REI SCRIPT FOR CSB #7

I shall now mentally picture myself in a situation where I normally think CSB #7, but I shall sincerely think: I refuse to worry anymore about this situation.'"* My worry just makes me unproductively miserable. I shall just do the things that I am willing and able to do to prevent my dreaded event from happening. Then, I shall rationally accept the results of my behavior. As I await those results, I shall keep myself rationally calm naturally with a warm, soft smile on my face and by breathing at my slow relaxing pace.

*Actually picture a specific troublesome situation in your mind and see yourself rationally refusing to worry about it. Instead, see yourself calmly dealing with it in the most rational way possible.

CSP's #14 and 15 may interfere with my corrective REI's for CSB #7.

CSB #8: I believe that people should live up to their potential.

HELPFUL FACTS AND INSIGHTS

Honest scores higher than 2 on CSB #8 often reveal people who hold irrationally arbitrary standards that are usually associated more with frustrations than with natural happiness in their lives.

MY PRESCRIBED REI SCRIPT FOR CSB #8

I shall now mentally picture myself in a situation where I normally think CSB #8, but I shall sincerely think: My performance is always up to my potential for what I actually do in any situation at the moment. Consequently, I always live up to my potential; I have no choice about that. When I don't perform as well as I desire, therefore, I shall rationally change that performing behavior and thereby increase my potential for better future performances.

CSB #9: I believe there is me and another "real me." (See CSB #9 in Chapter 13 for a complete discussion of this item.)

CSB #10: I believe my emotional feelings are more important than my thoughts for giving me useful self-understanding and helpful insights.

HELPFUL FACTS AND INSIGHTS

True believers in CSB #10 often do irrational gut thinking instead of rational brain thinking. Gut thinking means accepting or rejecting new ideas or behaviors mainly on the basis of whether or not the new ideas or behaviors feel right or wrong. But even factual ideas and correct behaviors feel wrong when they conflict with old personal beliefs, even old irrational beliefs.

MY PRESCRIBED REI SCRIPT FOR CSB #10

I shall now mentally picture myself in a situation where I normally think CSB #10, but I shall sincerely think: For healthy self-understanding and self-control, my sincere thoughts are always more important than my emotional feelings. Therefore, when I pursue problem solving and self-improvement, I shall act only on my rational brain thinking and protect myself from gut thinking and the Irrational Gooney Bird Syndrome it often causes.

CSP's #7 and 17 may interfere with my corrective REI's for CSB #10.

CSB #11:   I believe that people just have to be unhappy if there is no one around who really cares about them.

HELPFUL FACTS AND INSIGHTS

True believers in CSB #11 usually have a poor self-image. That's why they are willing to make themselves miserable simply because certain people are not perceptive enough to see any personal advantage in caring about them.

MY PRESCRIBED REI SCRIPT FOR CSB #11

I shall now mentally picture myself in a situation where I normally think CSB #11, but I shall sincerely think: Because I rationally care about myself, I can be very happy, even if no one else cares about me. That's why I give myself unconditional positive self-acceptance and calmly accept however much love or caring attention others choose to give me.

CSP's #6, 8, 12, 13, 17, and 25 may interfere with my corrective REI's for CSB #11.

CSB #12:   I believe that I am incapable of sexually satisfying members of the opposite sex, and it depresses me.

HELPFUL FACTS AND INSIGHTS

Your CSB #12 is correct, except for the belief that "It" depresses you. The "It-Monster" (a fact or event) *never depresses you. Only you* can depress you. Sexual arousal is merely a specialized emotional response; it fits the same A,B,C model that all normal human emotions fit. That fact makes it clear that the only person who can sexually satisfy any specific person is the individual him or herself. All other people (including you) can do is help or cooperate with others in their attempts to satisfy themselves sexually.

Sometimes your sexual partners may decide that they don't want your help in getting sexually satisfied, or some of your sexual partners may be too sexually naive to know and do what they must do to sexually satisfy themselves. In either case, it won't matter how skilled you are in helping people achieve sexual satisfaction, at those times your partners will not achieve it.

MY PRESCRIBED REI SCRIPT FOR CSB #12

I shall now mentally picture myself in a situation where I normally think CSB #12, but I shall sincerely think: I can't sexually satisfy anyone except myself. But I can and shall become as skilled as possible in helping cooperative partners satisfy themselves. I shall read books, attend lectures and classes, and learn the most enjoyable ways to help my partners sexually satisfy themselves in every mutually acceptable, nonharmful way.

CSP's #1, 2, 3, and 6 may interfere with my corrective REI's for CSB #12.

Author's Note: Many physically healthy women express a similar belief in CSB #12 with: "I believe that I am incapable of achieving sexual satisfaction, and it depresses me." (We can give this CSB the number 12-A.) Some additional helpful facts and insights for those women are: Sexual behavior is learned behavior. To decondition and recondition any behavior requires both the appropriate sincere new thoughts plus enough practice time to make the new behavior habitual. But it is possible for anyone (male or female) with a healthy body to achieve sexual satisfaction. So if you are physically healthy, dismiss as irrational the idea that it is impossible for you to achieve sexual satisfaction. Then read articles or books on how to relax, and let enjoyable sexual experiences happen to you.

MY PRESCRIBED REI SCRIPT FOR CSB #12-A

I shall now mentally picture myself in a situation where I normally think CSB #12-A, but I shall sincerely think: For all of my voluntary sexual experiences I shall only see in my mind's eye the sexually enjoyable scenes and imagine only the sexually pleasant feelings that I desire and that I shall see and imagine now.

Then do the ISRM as you mentally act out your REI script.

CSB #13:   I believe people must have goals and direction in their lives that are generally accepted as worthwhile before they can accept themselves.

HELPFUL FACTS AND INSIGHTS

Honest scores higher than 2 on CSB #13 usually indicates that people have problems with self-dislike and/or uncomfortable anxiety. They are afraid that the worth of their goals and the direction in their lives are not acceptable enough to others for them to be satisfied with themselves.

MY PRESCRIBED REI SCRIPT FOR CSB #13

I shall now mentally picture myself in a situation where I normally think CSB #13, but I shall sincerely think: I rationally choose to give myself unconditional, rational self-acceptance regardless of what other people think of me, my life's goals, or the direction of my life. Therefore, I shall use the ISRM to refuse to feel any more emotionally miserable than actually helps me cope best with my life.

CSP's #5 and 6 may interfere with my corrective REI's for CSB #13.

CSB #14: I believe that if people get to know the real me, they will not like me and that will be awful or terrible.

HELPFUL FACTS AND INSIGHTS

True believers in CSB #14 usually have a strong belief in their own inferiority or defectiveness as human beings. To get the approval and affection of others, true believers in CSB #14 believe they have to claim to have behavioral skills and interests that they don't have; those untrue claims are how these people try to keep their imagined, defective "real" selves hidden from other people.

MY PRESCRIBED REI SCRIPT FOR CSB #14

I shall now mentally picture myself in a situation where I normally think CSB #14, but I shall sincerely think: I am always the real me, regardless of the interests and traits I have, or I pretend to have. Therefore, anyone who likes me always likes me for my real self. And since my feigned interests and traits seem to be the only ones that consistently get me the social approval I want, I shall rationally make them my real interests and traits.

CSP #7 and 22 may interfere with my corrective REI's for CSB #14.

CSB #15: Regardless of people's attempt to deceive me, I believe that I can pretty well tell when they are thinking bad things about me.

HELPFUL FACTS AND INSIGHTS

True believers in CSB #15 usually are emotionally insecure and highly suspicious. In addition to holding CSB #15, these people often believe that they can and do control what other people think of them. Consequently, they waste time and emotional energy endlessly debating thoughts like these: By doing this, I can be sure that Tom and Mary will think the right thing about me. But then Sue and Lori may get the wrong idea; I can't let that happen. Oh, damn it, why do people have to be so hard to get along with?

But here's the painful irony about the people whose thoughts these true believers worry about the most. Usually such people are in one of these three, roughly equal sized groups: (1) They already think what the true believers in CSB #15 are trying to keep them from thinking; (2) they probably never would think what the true believers in CSB #15 are afraid they might think; or (3) they rarely even think about these true believers at all.

MY PRESCRIBED REI SCRIPT FOR CSB #15

I shall now mentally picture myself in a situation where I normally think CSB #15, but I shall sincerely think: Unless people tell me, I can never know what they think about me. But I can always know for sure how they behave toward me. As long as people behave toward me the way I want them to behave I shall be satisfied. And even if and when they stop their desirable behavior toward me, I shall calmly accept that fact and rationally end our relationship; that is, of course, if I fail to influence them to change back to their old desirable behavior.

CSP's #8, 12, 13, 25, and 26 may interfere with my corrective REI's for CSB #15.

CSB #16: I believe what "feels right" to me is the most important thing for me to consider in deciding how it's best for me to act and react. (See Chapter 12 for the discussion of CSB #16.)

CSB #17: Even if people are not pleased themselves, I believe they still should try to please other people.

HELPFUL FACTS AND INSIGHTS

People who score higher than 2 on CSB #17 usually appear to be super nice and genuinely concerned about the welfare of the other people in their lives. Objective observation, however, often reveals that their super niceness and ostentatious concern really are "velvet-lined psychological straitjackets" with which these true believers try to control the other people in their lives. These true believers try to enslave others with their syrupy niceness and smothering concern "for your own good."

Why are believers in CSB #17 so intent on controlling other people? Secretly controlling the other person or people in their lives is the only way these true believerers have learned to feel emotionally secure. So their seemingly gaudy "sacrifices" for others are not sacrifies at all; they are hard but secret, bargains, struck without the other people's knowledge, at the price of their personal freedom.

MY PRESCRIBED REI SCRIPT FOR CSB #17

I shall now mentally picture myself in a situation where I normally think CSB #17, but I shall sincerely think: I am both the most important person in the world to me and the only person whom I can please. On the other hand, as soon as other people become aware of me, I have an influence on them. But those people still control what and how much influence I have on them, so whether I succeed or fail to have the influence I want to have on others, I shall make sure that I rationally please myself in the meantime.

CSP's #11, 12, 13, 15, 17, 19, 22, and 25 may intefere with my corrective REI's for CSB #17.

CSB #18: I believe that it's my regrettable past that is causing my personal problems now. (See CSB #18, in Chapter 13 for the discussion of this item).

CSB #19: I believe that worry sometimes helps me.

HELPFUL FACTS AND INSIGHTS

Scores higher than 2 on CSB #19 usually reveal the self-made, proverbial "worry wart."

MY PRESCRIBED REI SCRIPT FOR CSB #19

I shall now mentally picture myself in a situation where I normally think CSB #19, but I shall sincerely think: The *only* thing worry helps me do is feel emotionally miserable. I have given up my belief in the magical powers of worry. That's why I shall calmly do what I am able and willing to do to achieve my goals; then, I shall calmly await the results of my efforts by doing the ISRM as often as I need it to keep my emotional cool.

CSP's #16, 21, and 26 may interfere with my corrective REI's for CSB #19.

CSB #20: I believe that people (including myself) ought to be punished when they don't behave the way they should.

HELPFUL FACTS AND INSIGHTS

Scores higher than 2 on CSB #20 almost always reveal people who have a Jehovah complex (see Chapter 10). Often they have chronic or frequent episodes of guilt; their guilt is their self-punishment for their real and imagined "I should have but didn't" or "I shouldn't have but did" behavior. (See NII #1, Chapter 10, for a detailed discussion of should-behaviors).

MY PRESCRIBED REI SCRIPT FOR CSB #20

I shall now mentally picture myself in a situation where I normally think CSB #20, but I shall sincerely think: I (like all normal people) always behave the way I should behave at the moment I do something. That's why I deserve all the positive and negative results of my behaviors. However, sane, intelligent people like me do not have to punish or even threaten themselves to get themselves to behave in their own best interest. So I refuse to do either of those things anymore.

NII's #4 and 5 and CSP's 18, 19, and 20 may interfere with my corrective REI's for CSB #20.

CSB #21: I believe it's natural and normal to be upset when things that are really important to me don't go the way they should. (See Chapter 12 for a detailed discussion of this item).

CSB #22: I believe that people who control their emotions don't really enjoy life; they are like robots.

HELPFUL FACTS AND INSIGHTS

True believers in CSB #22 are miguided people who strongly resist improving their emotional control. They usually excuse their undesirable emotions with the incorrect belief that because their undesirable behaviors are natural and normal, "That (meaning their undesirable behavior) is just me; therefore, I shouldn't change, because if I change, I won't be my normal and natural self anymore."

MY PRESCRIBED REI SCRIPT FOR CSB #22

I shall now mentally picture myself in a situation where I normally think CSB #22, but I shall sincerely think: I do *not* have the choice of not controlling my emotions. My only choice is whether I will control my emotions in miserable or in misery-free ways. By refusing to learn personally desirable emotioal control, I just force myself to behave in the most robotlike Irrational Gooney Bird way possible. I refuse to do that anymore. I now see that to be the spontaneously healthy and happy person that I want to be, I must practice controling my emotions rationally, until I am as spontaneously satisfied with myself as I want to be.

CSP's #14, 17, and 20 may interfere with my corrective REI's for CSB #22.

CSB #23:   I believe people are happiest when their emotions are spontaneous, free, and uncontrolled. (The solution for CSB #23 is the same as for CSB #22.)

CSB #24:   I believe that people have to feel guilty about their shortcomings and failures; otherwise, they are not worthwhile people; I mean, that type of person is some kind of psychopath.

HELPFUL FACTS AND INSIGHTS

True believers in CSB #24 usually have problems with excessive guilt; they also unwittingly or purposely teach their children to have similar problems with excessive guilt. That's the main reason irrational guilt and depression seem to "run" in families; it's consistently modeled and taught.

MY PRESCRIBED REI SCRIPT FOR CSB #24.

I shall now mentally picture myself in a situation where I normally think CSB #24, but I shall sincerely think: Sane, intelligent people can get themselves to perform better in the future without making themselves feel excessively guilty about their present or past failures. I'm both sane and intelligent; that's why I refuse to feel guilty about my failures anymore. Instead, when I fail, I shall recommit myself to Thomas Edison's insight and rationally get on with my life.

When asked, "Mr. Edison, is it true that you failed a hundred times before you finally succeeded in inventing the electric light bulb?" Mr. Edison supposedly replied, "No, I did not fail a single time; I succeeded in learning ninety-nine different ways *not* to try to make electric light bulbs."

CSB's #11, 17, 18, 20, and 22 may interfere with my corrective REI's for CSB #24.

CSB #25: I believe that how bad I feel when a loved one leaves me, or otherwise behaves undesirably, shows how much I really care about that person.

HELPFUL FACTS AND INSIGHTS

Ture believers in CSB #25 are very likely to get irrationally depressed about the unwanted breakup of a relationship. In addition, they often are afraid to initiate or participate in new relationships. They are afraid of "having to" go through the same old emotional pain if their new relationships break up.* That fear is based solely on the magical "It-Monster" explanation of how emotions occur. The logic is: "Since 'It' broke my heart this time, 'It' just might do it again."

*People often react to CSB #25 about their pets, especially when their pets die.

MY PRESCRIBED REI SCRIPT FOR CSB #25

I shall now mentally picture myself in a situation where I normally think CSB #25, but I shall sincerely think: I can and shall rationally control my emotions even though my loved ones leave me, or otherwise misbehave. My miserable emotions only prove that I am creating miserable emotions. Starting right now, therefore, I shall refuse to make myself feel any worse emotionally than actually helps me immediately cope best with my current situation, regardless of what my loved ones do.

CSP's #11, 12, 13, 17, and 20 may interfere with my corrective REI's for CSB #25.

CSB #26: I believe that being really sincere in my desires and really honest about my emotions are the most important factors in making things turn out the way I want them to turn out.

HELPFUL FACTS AND INSIGHTS

True believers in CSB #26 are very likely to get undesirably upset about their disappointments and failures. They believe they have been cheated when their sincere desires don't produce the results they wanted.

MY PRESCRIBED REI FOR CSB #26

I shall now mentally picture myself in a situation where I normally think CSB #26, but I shall sincerely think: In addition to being sincere in my desires, I shall also do everything that's necessary to make things turn out the way I want them to turn out. And if I succeed, they *shall* turn out the way I want them to. Why? Because everything to make them turn out the way I want them to will have been done. So they will have to and therefore should turn out that way.

CSP's #11, 14, 15, and 20 may interfere with my corrective REI's for CSB #26.

CSB #27:   I believe that my usual emotional responses to people and life's events are the only real, natural, and normal feelings for me to have, and I would not be the "real" me if I changed them.

HELPFUL FACTS AND INSIGHTS

True believers in CSB #27 make themselves mental slaves to their emotional feelings and they become emotional puppets on the whimsical strings of fate and other people.

MY PRESCRIBED REI SCRIPT FOR CSB #27

I shall now mentally picture myself in a situation where I normally think CSB #27, but I shall sincerely think: Yes, my usual emotional feelings are real, natural, and normal for me; but that does not mean that they are rational or good for me. I am now learning to control myself in the most rational manner possible. After enough practice those rational emotional feelings and actions will become as natural and normal for me as any of my undesirable ones now are. In addition, at that time my present, undesirable emotions will have become so abnormal and unnatural that I'll simply refuse to have them anymore.

   CSP's #7, 14, 15, 16, 17, and 20 may interfere with my corrective REI's for CSB #27.

CSB #28:   I believe that if I make an honest effort to do something and still fail at it, that means that I can't do it, or it just was not meant for me to have that success. (See in Chapter 13 for the complete discussion of this item.)

CSB #29:   I believe that if certain people would treat me the way they should, I could feel better about myself and accept myself better.

MY PRESCRIBED REI SCRIPT FOR CSB #29

I shall now mentally picture myself in a situation where I normally think CSB #29, but I shall sincerely think: Everybody is always treating me exactly the way he or she now should be, even though it is not what I wanted to see. But I shall still accept myself as misery-free naturally as I now think it's best for me to be; and I shall continually work to get people to treat me exactly the way I want to be. And when they refuse to cooperate with me, I shall ignore them in favor of people who happily comply with my behavioral desires naturally.

CSP's #8, 10, 12, 13, 20, 22, and 25 may interfere with my corrective REI's for CSB #29.

CSB #30:   I believe that if I could just make certain people see how their actions cause me such emotional pain, they would treat me better.

HELPFUL FACTS AND INSIGHTS

True believers in CSB #30 are most often frustrated parents and disappointed lovers. They make themselves feel emotially miserable about other people's behaviors; then out of emotional ignorance they put themselves and those other people in the following no-win situation: They sincerely but irrationally accuse other people of hurting them emotionally; then, like all emotionally naive, but sane, intelligent, hurting people, they demand that those other people at least stop hurting them. At best, they want these people to apologize and promise never to hurt them again, plus make them feel good now. But since those other people never were hurting these true believers in the first place, those other people can't stop hurting them.

MY PRESCRIBED REI SCRIPT FOR CSB #30

I shall now mentally picture myself in a situation where I normally think CSB #30, but I shall sincerely think: My own painful beliefs are the only things that can cause me emotional pain. Therefore, starting right now, I shall decrease my emotional pain immediately by refusing to believe ideas that will make me feel any worse emotionally than immediately helps me cope best with other people and my life in general.

The best way to get people to treat me better is for me to treat them better first. Therefore, starting today, I shall rationally improve *my* behavior toward the people from whom I want to get better treatment. But if after a reasonable period of time, they still do not treat me the way I want to be treated, I shall rationally accept that fact. Then, I shall immediately replace that relationship with a more personally satisfying one.

CSP's #8, 10, 12, 13, 19, 20, and 25 may interfere with my corrective REI's for CSB #30.

CSB #31: I believe that people have to love themselves in order to accept themselves.

HELPFUL FACTS AND INSIGHTS

True believers in CSB #31 usually believe that they are somehow unlovable. Because they don't like that idea, they often proclaim how they love themselves and how great loving oneself is for helping people accept themselves.

THE FACTS ABOUT SELF-ACCEPTANCE

It's impossible to remain sane and alert and not accept yourself. To refuse to accept something, including yourself, means to refuse to have anything to do with it; you must send it away or otherwise get away from it. Obviously, though, you can *not* send yourself away from you—everywhere you go, you are there. Therefore, since you cannot refuse to have anything to do with yourself, you cannot refuse to accept yourself.

Granted, you *can* go insane and have the delusion that you are someone else. But you will still be your objectively real, insane self, incorrectly believing that you are someone else. So let's face it, the only choice sane, alert people have about self-acceptance is how they do it—namely as miserably or as misery-free as possible. But they must *always* accept themselves, even though they passionately hate themselves.

MY PRESCRIBED REI SCRIPT FOR CSB #31

I shall now mentally picture myself in a situation where I normally think CSB #31, but I shall sinerely think: Instead of loving or hating myself, I shall always give myself unconditional, positive self-acceptance because I am always all I have and all I need to live my most personally satisfying life. To try to reject myself is both irrational and insane behavior, so I refuse to do that anymore.

CSP's #1 and 6 may interfere with my corrective REI's for CSB #31.

CSB #32:   I believe that there are universal standards of right and wrong that everybody should follow regardless of their personal feelings about them. (See Chapter 13 for a detailed discussion of this item.)

CSB #33:   I believe that everyone needs and has to be loved in order to accept him or herself.

HELPFUL FACTS AND INSIGHTS

Honest scores higher than 2 on CSB #33 often reveal what my good friend and mentor Dr. Albert Ellis calls "love slobs." Those people usually hate themselves so passionately that they believe that they can't stand "for a minute" to be alone, i.e., without a presumed loving mate. These are the people who naively believe "a bad love is better than no love at all." In reality, though, the only thing that a bad love is better than is a worse love. Often "no love" is infinitely better than a bad love.

MY PRESCRIBED REI SCRIPT FOR CSB #33

I shall now mentally picture myself in a situation where I normally think CSB #33, but I shall sincerely think: I am all I have and all I need to give myself is unconditional, positive self-acceptance and all the natural happiness that comes with it. Starting today, therefore, I shall give myself unconditional, positive self-acceptance by refusing to feel any more upset about anything than actually helps me cope better with it to my satisfaction.

CSP's #1, 3, 6, 10, 12, 13, and 25 may interfere with my REI's for CSB #33.

CSB #34: I believe that everyone ought to put other people's feelings ahead of his or her own feelings more often.

HELPFUL FACTS AND INSIGHTS

Honest scores of 3 or more on CSB #34 often reveal people who voluntarily make themselves victims of emotional blackmail. Emotional blackmail is when person A gets person B to act contrary to his or her desires simply because person A is, or threatens to become, emotionally upset if person B doesn't comply with person A's demands.

MY PRESCRIBED REI SCRIPT FOR CSB #34

I shall now mentally picture myself in a situation where I normally think CSB #34, but I shall sincerely think: People's emotional feelings are the products of their personal beliefs. Like most other people, when I want to put someone else's emotional feelings ahead of my own, that indicates that I have the magical and therefore irrational belief that I can control other people's emotions. People who know and use their emotional A,B,C's don't hold that irrational belief. That's why they rationally keep themselves safe from emotional blackmail.

I am a sane, intelligent person. That's why I rationally concern myself first and foremost with my own emotional feelings. But like all rational people, I shall rationally do what I'm willing to do to influence other people to feel as pleasant as possible in their relationships with me. Still, I shall always remember that people have the right to make themselves feel as miserable or as misery-free as they desire, for any reason they please.

CSB's #8, 10, 11, 12, 13, 17, 22, and 25 may interfere with my corrective REI's for CSB #34.

CSB #35: I believe that how other people treat a person is the main factor in determining how that person feels about him or herself and whether or not that person has a positive self-image.

HELPFUL FACTS AND INSIGHTS

That belief is quite valid for people who are below ten years old. Such people are normally naive and ignorant about the real meaning of their emotional reactions and physical behaviors, as well as about the meaning of the reactions they get from other people. It's easy to understand, therefore, why such young children base their self-images and emotional feelings about themselves largely on how other people seem to treat them.

But what if children are taught their emotional A,B,C's? Then they see that they can feel good about themselves, regardless of how badly other people may treat them. That fact makes teaching children their emotional A,B,C,'s one of the best things parents, schools, or any children's organization can do for the children.

MY PRESCRIBED REI SCRIPT FOR CSB #35

I shall now mentally picture myself in a situation where I normally think CSB #35, but I shall sincerely think: Regardless of how people treat me, the two things that I alone control are my emotional feelings about myself and my self-image. That's why I shall always remember that I have *the same human worth* that all other human beings have; in addition, I shall always rationally give myself unconditional positive self-acceptance because that is one of the most emotionally healthy things I can do for myself. And I honestly believe that I deserve the best of everything that I can give myself.

CSP's #8, 10, 11, 12, 13, and 24 may interfere with my corrective REI's for CSB #35.

CSB #36: I believe that magical powers are a factor in determining what happens in my everyday life.

HELPFUL FACTS AND INSIGHTS

There is no place for magical thinking in a healthy approach to human behavior. It is clearly self-defeating to blame magical powers for our everyday life experiences; that's why rationally thinking people refuse to do it.

MY PRESCRIBED REI SCRIPT FOR CSB #36

I shall now mentally picture myself in a situation where I normally think CSB #36, but I shall sincerely think: There is no objective reason to believe that magical powers exist outside my imagination. Therefore, I shall always rationally accept the events in my life as being the most logical results of my behaviors at those moments, and/or my habitual approach to life. When things in my life are different from what I want to see, I shall keep myself rationally calm naturally, while I do all I can to make those things exactly the way I want them to be for me.

CSP #15 may interfere with my corrective REI's for CSB #36.

People are social beings. That's why they usually learn most things best while they are participating in small supportive groups. That is especially so for learning improved emotional self-control. For that reason, I shall now introduce you to I-ACT (International Association for Clear Thinking) and strongly recommend that you contact this excellent organization.

I-ACT is an international nonprofit organization of people from all walks of life. Their common bond is their desire to cope better with life according to the basic principle of normal human behavior described in this book. For more information write: Mrs. Shirley Bender, Executive Director, I-ACT Headquarters, P.O. Box 1011, 3339 West Spencer Street, Appleton, Wisconsin 54911.

Figure 16–3. Headquarters of I-ACT

CHAPTER 1

1. False
2. False
3. True
4. (a) thinking; (b) reacting; (c) emotional; (d) physical
5. (a) self- ; (b) behavior
6. (a) thinking; (b) reacting
7. See page 5.
8. mental
9. True
10. False
11. They read self-help books as fast as possible, from front to back, without reviewing what they have read.
12. True
13. (a) write or make or take; (b) review
14. True
15. Trouble

CHAPTER 2

1. analyze
2. (a) yourself; (b) self-analysis
3. (a) unhappy; (b) self-justifying; (c) self-defeating
4. (a) erase; (b) replace; (c) perceptions; (d) irrational; (e) attitudes; (f) rational
5. False
6. False
7. (a) rarely; (b) rationality; (c) beliefs; (d) attitudes; (e) feelings
8. (a) pollutants; (b) beliefs; (c) distress
9. False
10. True
11. False
12. True
13. (a) two; (b) people or thinkers; (c) image; (d) concept
14. False
15. (a) four; (b) YUPI; see page 28.

CHAPTER 3

1. To prevent relapse into undesirable emotional states.
2. (a) diaphragm; (b) smile
3. (a) twelve; (b) fifteen
4. See page 40.
5. Genuinely smiling
6. False: Research shows that even smiles on request cause positive physiological responses.
7. See page 42.
8. See page 41.
9. I don't know of one.
10. False

249

CHAPTER 4

1. (*a*) never; (*b*) maintain;
   (*c*) beliefs; (*d*) attitudes
2. (*a*) words; (*b*) eyes
3. (*a*) emotions; (*b*) logical;
   (*c*) beliefs; (*d*) perceptions
4. think
5. (*a*) think; (*b*) feeling
6. feeling
7. thinking
8. When you are correct, your
   thoughts best fit the obvious,
   objective facts. When you are
   only right, your thoughts are
   logical and appropriate for your
   emotional feelings about the
   event in question, but not
   necessarily for that objective
   event.

9. (*a*) It-; (*b*) completely;
   (*c*) people's; (*d*) understand
10. See page 50.
11. (*a*) real; (*b*) right; (*c*) beliefs;
    (*d*) objective, or external, or
    obvious
12. False
13. False
14. (*a*) what you believe
15. (*a*) real; (*b*) words, or word-
    picture or word-thought

CHAPTER 5

1. (*a*) seem; (*b*) automatically
2. (*a*) attitudes;
   (*b*) superconscious; (*c*) It-
3. (*a*) jokes; (*b*) lies; (*c*) sincere or
   true
4. (*a*) A,B,C; (*b*) habits
5. (*a*) essential or necessary;
   (*b*) habit; (*c*) habit
6. (*a*) unspoken; (*b*) facts or
   realities; (*c*) better; (*d*) life

7. (*a*) Attitude; (*b*) react;
   (*c*) automatically; (*d*) thinking
8. (*a*) imagination; (*b*) It-
   Monsters; (*c*) feel or have
9. (*a*) learning; (*b*) self-protection
10. (*a*) Attitudes; (*b*) spontaneity;
    (*c*) improve

CHAPTER 6

1. (*a*) practicing; (*b*) reactions
2. (*a*) perception; (*b*) unspoken or
   silent; (*c*) unnoticed
3. perceptions
4. (*a*) Beliefs; (*b*) facts
5. (*a*) beliefs; (*b*) realities; (*c*) sane
   or rational
6. By reacting that way, I react as
   if I believe what?

7. (*a*) Attitude; (*b*) naive; (*c*) "It-
   Monster"
8. (*a*) Repetition; (*b*) learning;
   (*c*) emotional
9. (*a*) A,B,C; (*b*) practice or
   learning; (*c*) emotional or
   physical
10. Unspoken

CHAPTER 7

1. (*a*) real; (*b*) mind
2. (1) Those made with external sensory input from objective reality.
   (2) Those made mainly with your beliefs, self-talk, or imagination.
3. (*a*) fast; (*b*) easy; (*c*) reliable; (*d*) facts
4. (*a*) not; (*b*) believe
5. (*a*) believe; (*b*) experience or reality (either)
6. False
7. (*a*) never; (*b*) semantics; (*c*) always; (*d*) semantics

8. Would a videotape of my perceptions show what I said happened?
9. thinking
10. (*a*) incorrect; (*b*) common; (*c*) emotional
11. See page 89.
12. If "yes," that's great; immediately start doing it. If "no," then immediately reread the chapter.
13. I can't think of one.
14. Whatever you honestly say is okay for you.
15. Any sincere answer is okay.

CHAPTER 8

1. See pages 97 and 99.
2. False
3. (*a*) emotive; (*b*) third; (*c*) better
4. (*a*) Cognitive; (*b*) improvement or change or help; (*c*) give
5. (*a*) Cognitive; (*b*) dissonance; (*c*) almost; (*d*) solved

6. (*a*) Emotive; (*b*) practice or rehearsal
7. REI
8. (*a*) insight; (*b*) fourth
9. True
10. (*a*) REI; (*b*) real; (*c*) cognitive; (*d*) dissonance

CHAPTER 9

1. See page 117.
2. (*a*) Doing REI incorrectly or (*b*) not doing it often enough.
3. As long (i.e., as many weeks) as it takes you to get the instant and automatic reactions you desire, usually at least thirty days.
4. None at all
5. False
6. True
7. Act the way people act who already have that habit.
8. They cling to their old beliefs and attitudes.

9. They look alike to the casual eye.
10. They refuse to do self-helpful thinking when it would be helpful to them.
11. They unrealistically expect to get better emotional and behavioral results without thinking better.
12. True
13. See page 114.
14. (*a*) imagination; (*b*) emotional; (*c*) fastest; (*d*) safest; (*e*) way; (*f*) brains; (*g*) sincere; (*h*) objective

CHAPTER 10

1. (*a*) illusion; (*b*) real
2. (*a*) illusion; (*b*) toy, or rubber, or unreal; (*c*) real, or dangerous, or harmful
3. (*a*) forced; (*b*) physically
4. choice
5. (*a*) Jehovah; (*b*) *shoulds*
6. (*a*) Goodness or God; (*b*) Working; (*c*) sincere; (*d*) TGIF
7. (*a*) never; (*b*) everything, or something; (*c*) should
8. (*a*) *shoulds*; (*b*) *shouldn'ts*
9. (*a*) should; (*b*) want; (*c*) demand
10. (*a*) always; (*b*) should
11. (*a*) stay; (*b*) is
12. (*a*) rare, or seldom; (*b*) forced
13. (*a*) remind; (*b*) benefits; (*c*) them
14. choose
15. (*a*) labor; (*b*) themselves; (*c*) mouths; (*d*) them; (*e*) oldest; (*f*) normal
16. (*a*) drugs; (*b*) think or believe
17. (*a*) never; (*b*) emotional or self; (*c*) semantics
18. (*a*) joking; (*b*) lying; (*c*) brain; (*d*) experience, or subjective reality

CHAPTER 11

1. (*a*) believe; (*b*) Camera; (*c*) objective
2. See pages 142, 145, and 146.
3. Move on to the next NII or higly scored YUPI item.
4. To help you most rapidly personalize those ideas.
5. False
6. See page 143.
7. No
8. People are equally fallible; people vary only in the frequency of revealing that equality.
9. No
10. (*a*) sense; (*b*) inconvenient or undesirable; (*c*) inconvenient or undesirable
11. (*a*) three; (*b*) sciences; see page 125
12. (*a*) always; (*b*) now; (*c*) not; (*d*) wanted; (*e*) God; (*f*) willing; (*g*) do; (*h*) necessary; (*i*) things
13. They didn't do what was necessary to win.
14. Being physically overpowered and having no choice at all.
15. (*a*) choice; (*b*) forced
16. See page 135.
17. Any answer is acceptable
18. (*a*) perceive; (*b*) believe or think—either one
19. (*a*) joking; (*b*) lying; (*c*) beliefs
20. (*a*) true; (*b*) right; (*c*) emotional; (*d*) experiences

CHAPTER 12

1. See pages 152 and 155.
2. See pages 154 and 161.
3. False
4. (*a*) rationally; (*b*) four
5. Keep it, of course.
6. False
7. It means "my habitual behavior."
8. True
9. If you are having a habitual experience.
10. False
11. (*a*) Irrational; (*b*) syndrome; You are thinking with your gut instead of with your brain.
12. It helps you keep doing what you are doing that you want to keep doing.
13. (*b*) your rational brain thinking

CHAPTER 13

1. (*a*) camera; (*b*) rational; (*c*) rules; (*d*) thoughts
2. REI
3. (*a*) daily; (*b*) get, learn, or achieve; (*c*) better; (*d*) skill
4. True
5. (*a*) REI's; (*b*) life; (*c*) practice; (*d*) enough; (*e*) learn, get, or achieve; (*f*) better
6. (*a*) responsibility; (*b*) you; (*c*) I
7. (*a*) illusion, belief or idea; (*b*) two; (*c*) I, or rational; (*d*) you, or irrational
8. See page 168.
9. (*a*) seldom, rarely, or never; (*b*) self-control, or emotional control, or behavior
10. See page 167–168.
11. See page 172.

INDEX

255